The 2-Step Marketing Secret that Never Fails!

By **T.J. Rohleder**
(a.k.a. "The Blue Jeans Millionaire")

Other Great Titles from T.J. Rohleder:

Ruthless Marketing Secrets (Series)
Stealth Marketing
Instant Cash Flow
The Power of Hype
3 Steps to Instant Profits
Money Machine
The Blue Jeans Millionaire
How to Turn Your Kitchen or Spare Bedroom into a Cash Machine
The Black Book of Marketing Secrets (Series)
The Ultimate Wealth-Maker
Four Magical Secrets to Building a Fabulous Fortune
The Ruthless Marketing Attack
How to Get Super Rich in the Opportunity Market
$60,000.00 in 90 Days
How to Start Your Own Million Dollar Business
Fast Track to Riches
Five Secrets That Will Triple Your Profits
Ruthless Copywriting Strategies
25 Direct Mail Success Secrets That Can Make You Rich
Ruthless Marketing
24 Simple and Easy Ways to Get Rich Quick
How to Create a Hot Selling Internet Product in One Day
50 in 50
Secrets of the Blue Jeans Millionaire
Shortcut Secrets to Creating High-Profit Products
Foolproof Secrets of Sucessful Millionaires
How to Make Millions While Sitting on Your Ass
500 Ways to Get More People to Give You More Money

FIRST EDITION

ISBN 1-933356-97-9

Table of Contents

Introduction:

By T.J. Rohleder

THANK YOU for purchasing this book. As you'll see, you made a GREAT DECISION that could be worth huge sums of money to you! Because, in the first Chapter of this book, I'm going to show you how to get rich with the SAFEST and MOST PROFITABLE marketing strategy in the world! That's a tall order, I know. And I don't blame you for being skeptical about this. And, yet, as you'll discover in Chapter One...

'2-Step Marketing' is the SAFEST WAY that you can find, get, and keep MORE of the very best customers and clients!

Yes, there's NO SAFER and MORE PROFITABLE and MORE EFFECTIVE way to build your business than 2-Step Marketing and I'll prove it to you! So strap on your seatbelts and get ready for the ride! You're going to FALL IN LOVE with the awesome power that this simple, but totally proven marketing method can give you!

But wait, there's more!

You see, Chapter One is where I came up with THE TITLE of this book and you're going to be THRILLED to discover more about this powerful '2-Step Marketing Strategy' that can transform your business! And yet, the other chapters in this book are also powerful! Each of these additional chapters contains another powerful marketing strategy that I have used to build my own small business. **I can't wait to reveal these amazing secrets to you!** As you'll see—these methods have generated TENS OF MILLIONS OF DOLLARS in sales for my company and for many other people who are using them—and they can be worth a HUGE FORTUNE to you, too!

Remember, all the money you want, need, and deserve is out there WAITING FOR YOU—right now!

This money is in the wallets and bank accounts of the VERY BEST PROSPECTIVE BUYERS who are in your marketplace right now! All you have to do is find as many ways as you can to attract, then get and keep MORE of these very best customers and clients—and all the money you want is yours! Yes, it's this simple. It's NOT easy, and yet it is simple. And the more you understand about the game of marketing and all the things you can do to ATTRACT and RETAIN the very best prospective buyers, the more excited you'll be! As you'll see, this truly can give you THE COMPETITIVE ADVANTAGE you need to succeed beyond your wildest dreams! So please go through this book carefully and get my very best marketing secrets that give you the TOTAL POWER to find, get, and keep MORE of the very best customers and clients in your marketplace.

And to reward you for purchasing this book, I have…

A great FREE business-building gift for you!

Yes, I have a gift waiting for you that can DRAMATICALLY INCREASE YOUR SALES AND PROFITS! Here's what it's all about: I spent TEN FULL YEARS writing down all of the greatest marketing and success secrets I discovered during that time period. Each day, I took a few notes and, at the end of a decade, I had a GIANT LIST of 6,159 powerful secrets! This list is ALMOST 1,000 PAGES of hardcore money-making ideas and strategies!** **Best of all, this massive collection is now YOURS ABSOLUTELY FREE!** Just go to: www.6159FreeSecrets.com and get it NOW! As you'll see, this complete collection of 6,159 of my greatest marketing and success secrets, far more valuable than those you can buy from others for $495 to $997, is absolutely **FREE.** No cost, no obligation.

Why am I giving away this GIANT COLLECTION of secrets, that took ONE DECADE to discover and compile, FOR FREE? That's simple: I believe many of the people who receive these 6,159 secrets in this huge 955 page PDF document will want to obtain some of our other books and audio programs and participate in our special COACHING PROGRAMS. However, you are NOT obligated to buy anything—now or ever.

I know you're serious about making more money or you wouldn't be reading this. So go to: www.6159FreeSecrets.com and get this complete collection of 6,159 of my greatest marketing and success secrets right now! **You'll get this GREAT FREE GIFT in the next few minutes, just for letting me add you to my Client mailing list,** and I'll stay in CLOSE TOUCH with you... and do all I can to help you make even more money with my proven marketing strategies and methods.

THE 2-STEP MARKETING SECRET THAT NEVER FAILS!

So with all this said, let's begin…

** WARNING: This complete collection of 6,159 marketing and success secrets contains MANY CONTROVERSIAL ideas and methods. Also, it was originally written for MY EYES ONLY and for a few VERY CLOSE FRIENDS. Therefore, the language is X-RATED in some places [I got VERY EXCITED when I wrote many of these ideas and used VERY FOUL LANGUAGE to get my ideas across!] so 'IF' you are EASILY OFFENDED or do NOT want to read anything OFFENSIVE, then please do both of us a favor and DO NOT go to my website and download this FREE gift. THANK YOU for your understanding.

CHAPTER ONE

2-Step Marketing is the <u>safest</u> and most profitable way to make money.

STEP ONE: Attract a highly qualified prospect.

- Use a great offer.
- Don't try to sell them too much at first.
- Get your hooks into them.
- Make it as easy as possible for them to buy the first time.
- Sell a low-priced widget.
- Educate them.
- Make them feel that *"They came to you"* — and <u>not</u> the other way around.

STEP TWO: SLAM THEM!

- Now bring out the BIG GUNS!
- You already have their attention and interest... Now you are in the position to show them how you can give them what they desire.

Embrace Two-Step Marketing

Two-step marketing is nothing less than the safest and most profitable way to make money. It's simple: in Step One, you attract a highly qualified prospect. You use a great offer to draw them in, and you don't try to sell them too much at first. **This is how you get your hooks into them: you make it as easy as possible for them to buy or take some other action that first time.** Let's say you send them a free report, or sell them a low-cost widget of some type. **When they come back for more, this makes them feel like they're the ones coming to you, rather than vice-versa.**

In general, that's Step One: getting people to raise their hands. Step Two is where you slam them, as we like to say; it's all above converting as many leads as possible into sales. You're bringing out the big guns, because now you've got them. They initially responded to a small offer, **so now you're doing everything possible to educate them on the reasons why they need to buy whatever you ultimately want to sell them.**

Now, within that guise of simplicity, things can get very complicated. You can spend your whole life mastering the intricacies of this two-step formula, but when you boil it down to its basic constituents, it's very simple. **Yet this formula of drawing people in with small offers and then cashing in later with big ticket offers is responsible for God only knows how**

many hundreds of billions of dollars in sales every year. Two-step marketing is very common, and some people are doing it without even realizing it. Any time you do something to try to get somebody to take a simple step that will lead to bigger steps down the road, that's a form of two-step marketing.

The key to learning how to use this method effectively is to start paying close attention to all the two-step advertising that other people are using. Look at the things that marketers are trying to do to get somebody to take that initial step—whether it's to pick up a telephone, send for a free report, or come into the store. This is that first step marketers are trying to get new customers, or even established customers, to take. Start paying attention to this, and you'll see that some people are very, very good at it—while others are applying it haphazardly. **The more you become a serious student of two-step marketing, the more you're going to see common denominators, certain patterns that will help you hone your ability to create your own style of two-step marketing. Your goal should be to systematize all of this as much as you possibly can.**

Take our company, for instance. When business is humming right along, we've got an offer that's out there all the time, generating high-quality leads from people we've never done business with before—people outside our current customer base. We're making them a specific front-end offer, whether for low cost or for free. **The idea is to get them to raise their hands so we can convert them, and then cultivate them as a customer. Whatever we're trying to sell them later on is directly related to the front-end offer they responded to, so it's like a chip off of the bigger block of the whole offer, so to**

speak. Once they ask for it, you try to sell them the bigger block. In our current front-end campaign, we're ultimately trying to sell people 300 websites—but our first step is to make them an unbelievable bargain on 50 of those websites. We practically give those 50 websites away, so we can go back and try to sell them the other 250 in a bigger block. So, the front-end offer, the first step, is directly related to the back-end offer of the second step. **The more you're able to marry the two, the higher your conversion levels will be.**

Your goal in two-step marketing is to separate the smaller list of better-qualified prospective buyers from the larger list of prospects, that's all; and you're just trying to get them to take a small action. You're not trying to get people to do too much too fast; you're just trying to get them to take that initial step. **From that point forward, you're trying to get them to take the second step, which is to buy something more expensive so you can convert them into real customers. After that, you keep making them offers, hoping they'll come back again and again.**

We're testing a promotion right this minute for something we call our Direct Pay System. The first step is to get interested prospects to send for a free report and a free start-up manual. On top of that, we give them a fast-start audio CD and *then* five free bonuses, which are also on an audio CD. So in all, they get two audio CDs and a big package of information. **It's all theirs absolutely free; we're not asking for a penny.** That's the first step: people raise their hands, we send all this to them, **and *then* we try to sell them a very similar back-end offer than can amount to as much as $1,200.**

THE 2-STEP MARKETING SECRET THAT NEVER FAILS!

On that second step, where we attempt to convert the lead to the sale, we'll send as many as 10-30 follow-up postcards and letters. Each will try to get them to go ahead and take advantage of the larger thing we're trying to sell. **To make that conversion, you have to be relentless in your follow up.** You see, most people give up way too soon: they don't spend enough time, money, effort, or energy trying to convert those leads. They think that just because somebody who responded to that initial offer doesn't buy immediately, that person isn't interested.

Nothing could be further from the truth! We're living in a day and age in which apathy is alive and well; don't forget that. People are busy. They're bombarded; they're overwhelmed; they're confused; they're frustrated. **You've got to stay after these people and keep coming at them a little differently each time.** With our company, we don't just use direct mail; we also have our sales reps to call them to answer all their questions, to cover all the objections those people might have to buying. That's the one thing you can't do if you don't have salespeople: you're never going to find all the hidden objections that people have. **Even *with* salespeople, you might not identify all the real reasons… but you do stand a much better chance with them.**

And remember: all this is simple, when you get right down to it. **Any time you get confused by any of this, just go back to that simplicity.** It's all about generating leads, closing the largest possible percentage of those leads, and then continuing to do other kinds of marketing to sell them related products and services. Yes, it can be complicated; know that in advance. It's easy to learn, but it takes a lifetime to master, and you may never know everything there is to know. **Now, I don't want you to view that as a reason for depression; see it as a challenge instead.** Even though I may speak with total confidence about the subject, I'm still learning myself—and I love the challenge.

I happen to think that two-step marketing is a foundation principle of DRM; it's certainly one of those areas that's important to your success in the field. There are all kinds of things you could do to advertise your business: different directions you can take, different media you can use, and lots of different options within those categories. **But, the surefire, safest, and most profitable way to make money is to *first* attract highly qualified prospects and then do as much business with them as you can.** That's the simple strategy here, though again, it can cover a lot of different angles, a lot of different twists. There are many different things you can do within that broader concept. But if your goal in your business is always first to attract qualified prospects and then sell those prospects not just once time but many times, and to establish a long-running, profitable relationship with them, then you're on the right track.

It doesn't always work, of course, but that doesn't mean it's the wrong strategy. There may be times that your promotion doesn't succeed, or when other things aren't clicking; **but generally speaking, two-step marketing is the safest, most profitable long-term way to build your business and make lots of money.** You've got to start by having a deep understanding of your marketplace and the people who comprise it, the problems they're facing and need solved, the kinds of things they want as well as need, the challenges they're faced with; and then you've got to use a great offer to attract them to you and get them to raise their hand, to get them to want to do business with you in the first place.

Earlier, I mentioned our current main offer for new customer acquisition. **We're using this two-step marketing strategy to basically give away something that's extremely valuable.** We could sell the item for a goodly sum; and we know that some people might argue that we're giving it away way too cheaply. **But you see, we want to use an irresistible offer to attract the people that we want to become customers for life.** Since our ultimate goal is to attract the right kinds of qualified prospects for our main offer, we're willing and able to give away those valuable items, *knowing* that we're losing money that we could make on that initial sale. We do have a small one-time setup fee, but everything else is given away free, and we do that realizing that we're passing up on some money that we could make on the front-end... **but in so doing we're attracting a qualified prospect that we *know* is going to be interested in our main offer, since they're responding to a very similar free offer.**

We're holding that out there to get them to respond right away. We want the biggest possible number of people that we mailed that initial offer to to respond; when they do, they go on our prospect list. **When we market to that list, we know we'll get a much higher response rate than if we made the offer directly to the general public.** Of course, we get varying results on our mailings, and that's always one of the hardest questions to answer when people ask: they want to know what results you can expect from a mailing of a certain size, and we can't really tell them, because it fluctuates by a surprising amount. We never make any kind of guarantee regarding response rates, because we know if we did, someone might say, "Well, you told me that I would get *this* percentage of response rate. Just because you're getting that, I should get it, too." We don't want to run into those kinds of problems. The reality is that our numbers are all over the place. They're semi-consistent, but not so much that we can rely on them to be a benchmark.

We have a certain number of new customer acquisitions mailings we do on a weekly basis, and when our response rates come in, we look at those numbers. That's Step One. Based on that, we have a group of people with which to perform Step Two, which is to try to get as many of those people to become customers as possible. There's a clever, certainly unique formula for how to maximize your profits using this two-step marketing system, and **we call it "meet, convert, upgrade and expand."** The first part is to *meet* the right prospects, whether that's through contacting people by mail or with an ad, or actually meeting them in real life if you do door-to-door sales or have a brick-and-mortar store. These are the people who are most likely to want what you have, who will give you the maximum amount of money for the longest period of time.

The second part is converting those prospects: you want the biggest possible number of those people that you've met to become first-time buyers. You need to make it as easy as possible to get them to do business with you that first time. As long as they're qualified prospects, you want to get as many of them up and over the hurdle to raise their hand and make a first-time commitment, **to buy from you *once*.** At this point, you don't worry about building a lifelong customer; you just want them to respond the first time. **Once you have them solidly hooked, though, you then try to upgrade.** Make them your biggest and best offer, trying to separate the most serious prospects from the rest. **Get them while they're hot, and sell them as much as you can, as fast as possible.**

Approach them and say, "I know you bought Item A, so I think you might be interested in Item B, Item C, etc." **You're in a relationship now, so you're letting them know that there are other products and services, other opportunities to do more business with you that they need to take advantage of.** You're upgrading that relationship, taking it to the next level. Once you've converted and upgraded them, try to expand and extend the relationship with the customer for as long as possible. **This involves staying in close touch with them, creating a close bond of friendship, an ongoing relationship where you're selling them as much stuff as you can along the way, for as long as you can.** In so doing, you're creating a lifetime of revenue from all the repeat business you do with them. **You're creating a small group of core customers that you stay in constant contact with, because you know you can depend on them to buy what you're selling on a regular basis.** These are the best-of-the-best, your preferred customers, the clients you do business with the most. They're the ones you invite to all your preferred customer events; they're the ones you know you're going to see repeatedly in your store, or who will respond repeatedly to your offers if you're online or doing business by mail.

So, expand that business for maximum profits, not only at

the beginning of the relationship. **As you go on, you're seeking long-term profits from these clients.** You're seeking a relationship that continues to be rewarding over the lifetime of your business-client relationship. **Meet those prospects, convert them the first time, upgrade them, and then expand that relationship.** That's a very simple four-point formula for doing two-step marketing. **It's the safest and most profitable way to make money—not only now, but in the long term.** It's also the cheapest way to make money, in the long run; and, yes, it can be *very* challenging. There are many different variations on those two steps, and you can spend years learning how to work it in all its varying aspects. **But over time, it'll become second nature to you.**

CHAPTER TWO

Wisdom from a Master Showman:

"It's not the audience who has the power — it's me! It is my talent and ability to know how to keep giving them what they want. I am in control — not them."

— *Johnny Carson*

This is a paradox:

YES, the market comes first. But it's your ability to "read" the market to discover the most powerful and profitable ways to serve it that counts.

The power is in your hands, not theirs.

Wisdom From a
Master Showman

During an interview that Johnny Carson gave about 20 years before he died, he said, "It's not the audience who has the power—it's me! It is my talent and my ability to know how to keep giving them what they want. I'm in control—not them." When I read that, I realized what a great truth that is. I hope you realize it also. **Now, this statement may seem to be paradoxical, since we usually say that it's all about the market... but really, it's about our willingness and ability to give the market what it wants.**

To make all the money that you'll ever need, all you have to do is create the right idea for the right group of people, and then present it to them in the right way, and simply get enough of those people to give you enough money at enough profit per transaction to cover your cost of doing business with them, and presto! There it is. You don't have to go to business school. You don't have to get a master's degree, or any of that. It's really simple, and yet within that simple framework there are a lot of decisions to make. Johnny Carson hit the nail right on the head here. **"It's your talent."** He's saying it's *not* the audience (or in our case the market) that has the power. It's you! **It's your knowledge of how to keep giving them what you know that they want. So you're in control, not them.**

THE 2-STEP MARKETING SECRET THAT NEVER FAILS!

In some ways, we're all performers. My definition of selling ten years ago was that "selling is serving." I still believe there's some truth to that, but servants are not very well-paid people, are they? The highest-paid people are performers. **Therefore, my current best definition for selling or marketing is** *performing*: **your ability to give people what you know that they want, to serve it up bigger and better than all your competitors, to be the very best in your market.** That's the kind of spirit and bravado and attitude that Johnny Carson had—to be the very best in your market.

And let me repeat something you may be tired of hearing: **you really have to know who the people who make up your marketplace are.** You have to know them at an intimate level, better than they even know themselves. What are they really searching for? What drives them and compels them to buy the kinds of things that you and your competitors sell? You have to keep asking that question. Don't just be satisfied with superficial answers. **Go below the surface. What are they** *really* **looking for?** In a perfect world, if you had godlike superpowers and you could give them anything you wanted, without worrying about legal, moral, or ethical issues, what would it be? Ask yourself that. **Start writing down the answers; you'll get closer to the truth the more you think about it, the deeper you go.**

Study your market. Which competitors are delivering what people want in the biggest and best ways? Who's out there making the most money? Creativity does not happen in a vacuum. **You create by starting with a whole lot of pieces to create with.** It's like having building blocks, and part of that collection of blocks is understanding the market, knowing what's working well for others, knowing what's worked well for you in the past—anything that you can do to understand who these people are. **Then you've got to give them a performance; you've got to excite them.** We're dealing with an overcrowded, over-competitive marketplace where the average consumer is jaded. The same things that used to turn them on don't turn them on anymore. It takes more and more to get them jazzed, to get them excited, to get them enthusiastic. Don't let that discourage you; let that *challenge* you. Look at this challenge as a good thing, because it spurs you to work hard and be your very best..

In a nutshell, our job as marketers is to transmit the right offers to the right people through the right media. It's our ability to do that that's central, not the market. We don't serve the market. We're not servants here, we're high paid performers. **What matters is your talent and the ability to keep giving them what they want.** When Johnny Carson pointed this out, he was saying that his ability to be a good performer was predicated on his knowledge of what the audience wanted, and his ability to keep giving it to them. That's a great analogy for what it takes to be successful in business, which is why I always talk about the desires of the marketplace coming first.

If you're an inventor and you create a widget of some kind, you may spend your life savings and countless hundreds or thousands of hours designing and modeling and inventing this new item, whatever it does; and perhaps then, and only then, you go out and figure out who might be interested in buying it. When you come at the process from that angle, then you end up with a situation where you might not even know who your marketplace is. Oh, you might have an idea of the kinds of people that would be interested in responding to or doing business with you, but it might be fragmented; you might not have a clear idea of who would buy the item, who your ultimate customer is going to be. **On the other hand, if you start with a focus on the marketplace, then you can discover what those people want the most—and then and only then do you develop products and services that give them exactly what they want.**

So it starts with asking yourself these questions: What do these people want to buy? What problems do they have? What do they need solutions to? What struggles do they have? What challenges are they facing? And then you answer those questions. Solving those problems, addressing those concerns that people have, is your way to riches: your way to cracking the safe in your marketplace. **First, the market; and *then* the product or service.** In the previous section, I talked at length about the value of the 5:00 AM Club; and you'll recall that I talked about the marketplace there, too. This is how you know what to do when you're up that early in the morning. **It's all about focusing on the marketplace so you can figure out what they want, and then spending all of your time trying to find ways to give them those things.**

Once some people have developed a product they think, "Okay, what do I do now? I sit back and make the money, right?" Well, it's great to have one product—but then what's next? **You have to constantly be in search of the next great idea, or the next great product, or the next great service.** What are going to give them next? What do they want that you can *also* give them that's related to what they've already bought from you the first time? **By deeply understanding and serving your marketplace, you can develop a profitable relationship with them.** You can develop an understanding of them that lets you keep finding ways to provide the valuable services and products they want.

As Johnny Carson pointed out, **it's your talent and ability to know how to keep giving them what they want that really matters.** That's your goal as a marketer, and ultimately, it's what will determine your success or failure. **So the formula here is simple: first identify the marketplace, and then keep finding ways to give them what they want.** That puts the power in your hands, because you're not relying on this arbitrary process of throwing a product out there and hoping that enough people want it that you can make a profit somehow. **No, you *start* with the marketplace.** Because you've done your research, and you've crafted something to their demonstrated specifications, you know that they're going to be interested in it at some level.

Of course, that doesn't mean that every product or service that you offer will make a profit. But by knowing your market, and creating the kinds of things they like, you'll be closer to profit then you've ever been using any other method. **This process puts you in a position to be more confident in your ability to sell things that they want to buy. You're giving them solutions to their problems, answering their questions or concerns, providing solutions.** That's what this Johnny Carson quote was all about. First and foremost, it's your job as a marketer to give the people what they want; and to do that, you have to *know* what they want. It's as simple as that.

CHAPTER THREE

Creativity comes from the labor of a driven and highly determined person!

Rebelliousness is also a key factor to creativity.

- Think outside the norm of your industry.

- Question everything.

- Be an independent thinker.

- Strive to be different!

Conformity breeds people who are as creative as a head of cabbage!

The Origin of Creativity

"Creativity comes from the labor of a driven and highly determined person." This is a secret that I learned from a man named Gene N. Landrum, who has written about a dozen really good business books. I want you to think deeply about this quote.

Realize, too, that rebelliousness is a key factor in all creativity. You've got to think outside the norm of your industry. You've got to question things. You've got to be an independent person. You've got to be different. **A lot of marketing is about differentiation — that is, trying to do things to separate yourself from everyone else.** The best way to be creative is to be a rebel, and here's why: if you think about who a rebel is, who is their opposite number? It's someone who conforms... a follower. Followers don't question very much; they just follow. They're not radical. They're not rebellious. They're not independent. They need to be told what to do, and they strive to be the same at all times. They want to blend in. That's what they're all about.

Now, I'll admit that sometimes rebels tend to just follow other rebels, and they all look alike. There *can* be that same quality of conformity in somebody who considers himself to be a rebel. **But a rebel is typically somebody who *does* question things.** They ask "why" a lot. Little kids are creative as hell, because they have this quality. Chris Lakey has six of them now, and sometimes it seems that the only thing they ever ask is "Why? Why? Why? Why? Why?" They're hungry for knowledge. They want to *know*. And if you give them an answer, then they say, "Why?" If you give them another answer, they say, "Why?" again. They're questioning things, a key component to creativity.

The cousin questions here are, "Why not?" and "Why not me?" You've got to ask those questions to break out of the box of conformity, which is utterly necessary for success because conformity breeds people who are about as creative as a cabbage. **To be creative, you've got to be audacious. You've got to be different.** We talk about a unique selling position (USP) being very important in marketing. Well, it *has* to be, although it can't be too unique, because you've still got to work within a certain framework here.

A good metaphor would be the world of music. We've all listened to rock-'n-roll bands where every song contains the same three or four chords. That's because they know they have to stick within that success framework. They've got to keep giving people what they want again and again. **But within your marketing framework, you've still got to strive to be different, and you've got to do things that are a little controversial.** For example, tomorrow (as I write this) we're doing a teleseminar, and during that teleseminar we're going to show people how they can get $110,995 worth of websites that we've developed absolutely free... if they simply meet a certain condition we have.

Think about that. Over *$110,000 worth* of free websites,

and we're going to prove to them that those websites are worth it. **It's bold. It's audacious. It has to be, because the competition is more fierce that ever.** It's an overcrowded marketplace, and the average consumer is so resistant to sales messages that they don't believe anything anymore. You've *got* to do things to shock people. **You've got to be different if you're going to be noticed, and you've got to step outside of that line and not worry so much about what other people think.** Followers are locked into conformity, and part of conforming is never sticking your head out, never trying to be different, always being a blender.

In the marketplace, there are too many blenders. Everybody's following the follower. **Oftentimes, the people who make it are the ones that just have enough courage or audacity to just break out.** Again, it's a performance, as we talked about last time. It's also the essence of all creativity. So think "rebelliousness"—rebelliousness in a good way, where you question everything. You challenge different assumptions; you're trying to be independent as you possibly can, and you're not afraid to be different. **Then set huge goals, and don't try to figure everything out at once.** Remember: "Concepts first, details last" is one of the enduring principles that I teach.

Part of the essence of creativity is mixing a lot of different concepts together without getting bogged down in the actual details—never getting stuck or trying to think things through too much in the very beginning. **Just think conceptually.** Set huge goals, and fight. When you think of a rebellious person, you think of a fighter. When you think of somebody who's the opposite of that, you think of somebody who's passive. **You**

can't be passive. Business is war, and don't let anyone tell you any different.

You see, there are only so many people out there in your marketplace; there's only so much disposable income. If you're not out there trying to get all of it you can, there are plenty of other people who will be. **To succeed, you've got to fight and beat these people. You've got to be better than them, different from them.** Be audacious; question things. **All of that comes from being a driven and highly determined person.**

Some people are more driven than others, no question about it. But what a lot of people don't realize is that their drive comes from somewhere. Some of these driven entrepreneurs are making up for screwed-up childhoods, maybe. Could be that they got the crap beat out of them every day on the playground at school. Maybe some of that is true, **but what's also true, and more important, is that most of the truly driven entrepreneurs just have huge goals.** They've got big dreams, big visions. They're trying to pull something off in a big way, and they're serious about making those goals happen. That's part of what drives them. **So be creative and work toward the huge goals you've set—the bigger the better.** You may not always achieve them, but you'll probably do better than you ever have before.

And it does take a lot of creativity, which admittedly is one of those abstracts that you can't really nail down or quantify. You just see it, and you recognize it, and you strive for it. But it does come out of a determined place. **Creativity happens mostly when you take massive action to get somewhere.** Think about the people who aren't creative at all; they're unmotivated and not driven in any way. I think the way that you get creative is to be highly driven and determined to succeed. **When you take massive action, your creativity comes through in the process.**

Earlier, I touched on how creative children are. Think of how kids are with coloring books. Or you can just give a kid a piece of paper, and ask them to draw whatever's on their mind, and that creativity really emerges. All the ideas in their heads about life and the way things are come out in this creative process, which is limitless, because they neither worry nor care about how good their work is. They're not trying to win awards. **But as we reach adulthood, things change for us.** A lot of us get stuck in a job doing the same task over and over again. **Our creativity wanes, because we never have the ability to be creative.** There's no room for that, so we lose that creativity.

One of the reasons I believe rebelliousness is a key to creativity is because rebels tend to question everything. They tend not to take what people say at face value. When most people are told, "This is the way things are," they just accept it. They assume that that must be true, and then they move on, adjusting their lives accordingly. You could pass a law that's completely silly, and people will accept it. There are whole websites filled with all the silly laws on the books, many of which are no longer enforced. Most people are just going to go about their day, and they'll obey the law, and they won't ever question why that law exists.

Chris had a situation actually come up this past week where he contacted his congressman, and asked them to change a law that he thought wasn't right. It happened to be a tax law —

nothing real serious, but a tax law that affected Chris. The State Department of Revenue said that he owed them more money, because they said that he wasn't accounting for a certain part of the tax code. So Chris contacted his congressman; and when they meet at their next session, they're going to work on crafting legislation that will change the way the tax code is written. We'll see what happens. The end result is out of Chris's hands because he's not a legislator, but hopefully things will change.

I think Chris has a good reason for arguing the way he's arguing. He didn't accept that law when he first found about it. He's stuck right now having to pay the tax, because he's got no other recourse at this point. And yet, he's going to try to get that law changed. **That's basic to what I'm talking about here: the ability to question things, the ability to ask why things are.** I've talked about kids asking "why" all the time, and I see that regularly. Chris's three-year-old is in a phase where he wants to know why, and he wants to know your name. And so anytime he sees you, even though he knows you, even if you're a friend of the family, he will ask you what your name is. And then he'll ask, "Why?" And he'll ask what you're doing. So he questions. He's always asking questions. That's the inquisitive mind of a three-year-old.

And I think that creativity, the ability to ask questions, the ability to challenge your thinking, is an important part of the creativity process. It's about being driven for a certain purpose, for a certain goal that you have in mind—a certain challenge you're trying to meet. **Questioning everything, and constantly trying to break things and fix them in a better way, stems from that.** You have to try to push beyond the bounds of what's acceptable or possible. Now, I'm not talking about doing risky things, where you push the bounds of acceptable and decent human behavior. I'm talking about how this all relates to your business.

It's kind of like trying to break the sound barrier: like trying to fly faster or farther than anybody else ever has. It's like trying to run a mile faster than it's ever been done, or swimming some vast lake. It's trying to break the bounds of what people believe to be possible. **That's what the process of creativity is about: just trying to go beyond what's been done before, trying to come up with something new and different. You don't just accept the status quo;** you don't continue to accept that things have to keep being the way they that are, just because it's the way that they *have* been.

This sets the table for your creative juices to get flowing; and from that, I think, success is born.

CHAPTER FOUR

WE MUST BUY EVERY SALE WE MAKE!!!

✓ We are in the business of buying sales at a profit!

✓ We must constantly spend our money in proven ways that allow us to buy these sales at a profit.

Every new customer must be won! We must do something <u>BOLD</u> to attract them to us.

We Must Buy Every Sale We Make!

I didn't really learn this secret until I'd been in the business for about eight years, and I got it out of a direct marketing book by a fellow named Bob Stone. Stone was talking about one of his clients, about buying sales at a profit. That's when it hit me: **buying sales at a profit is the business that *all* of us are in!** I kind of knew that, but it hadn't been clearly articulated until that point.

When Eileen and I got our start back in late 1988, we were just babies in the business. **But one thing we did was take 30% of every single dollar that came in and put it into more new customer acquisition advertising.** We did this religiously. We had a separate advertising checkbook, and each day, we deposited 30% of our income into that account. That was the budget I got to spend on advertising. **So we were already doing it, without understanding fully what we were doing.** I'd never thought about that way before, but I immediately realized the truth of it.

You must constantly spend your own money on all the proven ways that allow you to buy those sales at a profit. Every customer must be won. **You've got to do something bold to attract them; and oftentimes, you have to be willing to spend a lot of money in the process.** To put it bluntly, your real success often comes from your ability to outspend your competition. You see, most of your competitors are just like those that P.T. Barnum, the great marketer who lived well over a hundred years ago, dealt with. He used to say, "Most people want to catch a whale by using a little, tiny minnow for bait."

With the Internet, you see this all the time. Everybody's looking for ways to get traffic to their websites for next to nothing. Well, some of them do end up with huge mailing lists, but those lists are generally worthless, because they're just random names. **They're not targeted toward people who actually buy their kinds of products. They're all trying to make a lot of money by spending a tiny bit of money.** Unfortunately, it doesn't work that way, for the most part. It does happen every now and again, but usually it costs money to make money. So you've got to be willing to spend that money.

Back in 1994, we started working with a famous marketer, and he produced some infomercials for us. We tested them in 14 different cities. We were selling an expensive item, and we got leads; but we just couldn't convert them to sales, which is an age old problem for us and for most marketers. **When he looked at everything we were doing, he simply said, "You're giving up on them too fast."** No matter how much I tried to reason with him, he kept saying that. "You're giving up on them too soon, TJ."

What he meant by that was that we just weren't putting enough pressure on those people. We weren't staying in touch with them enough, we weren't applying enough pressure, we weren't sweetening the offer enough for them, we weren't coming at them a million different ways with different offers, like we do now. Today, we don't give up on people easily. **If you send for something, say on a low-cost or a no-cost lead generation offer, we follow up. We're relentless.** We've got long form sequential mailings, we use a lot of direct mail, and we've got a sales department that also follows it up.

Admittedly, direct mail is very expensive—and so is employing a sales department that we manage ourselves, through a professional sales manager on our staff. **But again, it's not about what something costs, it's about the profit it makes you.** Oftentimes, the way to make more is to spend more. Now, you can go bankrupt thinking this way, and some people do. But for every marketer who goes bankrupt by spending too much money, there are many more who are struggling financially or going out of business because they're trying to use the *opposite* approach. They're trying to make money without spending money... and so they have no systematic way for attracting new customers, doing more business with the customers that they have, or continuing to develop new offers. **They look at everything as an expense, when they should look at their marketing as an investment towards future profits.**

One of the big advantages of direct response marketing is that you can track everything—it's not a big guessing game, like so many other types of advertising are. **You can easily figure out what's making you the most money, and then put more of your money back into those things.** That's how you buy these customers. You've got to spend some money.

For example, we've got a plan right now for selling a consulting program for almost five grand. **Part of our plan is to ensure that it's got other ways of making us money, too; so once we get those people into this consulting program, we have other ways to do business with them.** Each $4,985 sale is a gateway to *more* sales... and because of that, we're willing to spend $4,000 to make each initial sale. **Just think of the logic behind that example. That's the kind of thing you need to do to utilize this principle to its fullest.** A lot of people will go after that same $5,000 sale, but they might only want to try to spend a few hundred dollars to get it. They're not going all out and being serious.

When I say that your success can be dependent on your ability to outspend your competition, that's what I mean. If we're going head to head with one of our competitors who also has a $5,000 product, but we're willing to spend up to $4,000 to make that $5,000 sale while they're trying to spend a few hundred dollars, then who's going to be more successful? Who's going to make more sales? Who's going to build the bigger customer base? We are. We're going to win.

Now, this method isn't always easy to implement, but it's simple to understand. It requires you to get your mind into the right place, though. **You have to be willing to spend money to make money, and to think in terms of sales.** I would be as bold as to say that all marketing is about selling; instead of calling ourselves marketers, we should probably just call ourselves salespeople. **And what does it take to sell somebody? Among other things, it requires relentlessness.** You've got to be like one of those little bulldogs that just grabs ahold of a pant leg and won't let go. They're relentless. That's the way the best salespeople are, too. They're pushy; they're aggressive; they just keep coming at you from all directions until you break down and buy.

That's the way your marketing has to be, and one of the ways of being relentless—the way you finance that relentlessness — is to be willing to spend money. **You take a portion of your profits and put it back into more of the things that made you those sales to begin with. You commit yourself to the process of being willing to outspend other people.** When you have that mindset, and you're able to do things like I suggested in my example, you can be so aggressive and so bold and so relentless, because *now* you've got the money to back it all up. With money comes choices that you don't have when you're trying to do things without it.

Now, I'm pretty sure that the concept of buying every sale is foreign to most people, even within the marketing field — where people are supposedly trying to do everything they can to make a profit. That's sad, because it's an important strategy, which is why I've dedicated a whole chapter to it. It probably deserves even more space than I have to give it, because I truly believe that people don't think about their businesses this way. They think, "Well, I've got a product that I'm trying to sell, and here's what I'm doing to advertise, and orders are coming in, and I know that my company is making this much profit in the last quarter. We did this much business, and had this much expense, and hopefully we made a profit." That's the way they think about it, and it really doesn't get much more specific than that.

Direct response marketers are better at this. Yes, most direct response marketers understand that when you have a promotion, you mail a certain number of sales letters out, and your cost was this much, and then you've got this many orders, and then this was your profit. **You compare the expenses required to make the sale against the total dollar amount that you've made,**

and the difference is your profit on this particular mailing.
You do that over and over again, and you have yourself a
business. But when they're doing it right, direct response
marketers at least have some kind of reference point for this
strategy, and this is it. **We know we have to buy each and
every sale we make.**

**We hope that we're buying them at a profit, though that
might not immediately be the case.** In some cases, it's even
possible to build a thriving business despite losing money when
buying that first sale. Let's take the cell phone industry as just
one example. Let's say I go into my local cell phone store, and I
decide that I want the latest and greatest wireless device. Today,
as I write this, in my opinion that happens to be the iPhone. So I
walk into the Apple store to pick up an iPhone, and attach it to
AT&T for wireless service.

They're not going to charge me the $600 or $700 required
to make the iPhone; instead, they're going to take a hit on that
initial sale. They're going to charge me $200 to take this phone
home today. But they know they're going to make a profit in the
end! **Sure, they've lost several hundred dollars just to get
that phone into my hands, but they're buying a customer.**
They're willing to lose money on that initial sale because over
the course of that two-year contract, I'm not only going to pay
back the cost of the phone (because I'm paying for monthly
service), but hopefully I'll buy ring tones and other things from
them. Maybe while I'm a good AT&T mobile phone customer,
I'll sign up for home phone service, get TV through them, or any
number of other Internet services, or make some other purchase
that will add to their profitability.

They will have bought me as a customer, and hopefully will be making profits into the future. That's how it works in the cell phone industry: they're buying every sale that they make. DirecTV does it also. They give away their equipment, or maybe they charge $100 for the equipment when you sign a one- or two-year agreement. They've lost money making that sale to you, and will make it up selling you things like NFL Sunday Ticket, the baseball package if you want to watch baseball games, or even just from you watching pay-per-view movies. **That's buying a sale. They do that over and over. That's how they can spend billions buying customers, yet still earn a profit from them.**

Of course, you don't *have* **to lose money buying a sale. In fact, you can break even or make money acquiring a customer.** The important thing is to be willing to spend money to get those customers, because it's hard to get them otherwise. **If you're serious about the business and you're doing consistent new customer acquisition, it's going to cost you money to make money.** That's just the way it is. You have to account for that as part of your business model... and you have to think of it in the right way for it to work for you. Let's say you have a business model where it costs you $1,000 to advertise, and you brought in $1,000 worth of sales. Some people would be aghast at the expense, given that there was zero profit. **But think of it this way: you just got all those customers essentially for free. Now you can really start making money!**

On the other hand, if you spent $1,000 and made $1,500, well, you did buy customers, but you made $500 doing it. On flip side, if you spend $1,000 to run the ads or do the mailing and only got back $750 in business, well, you spent $250 to buy all those customers. That's how you have to look at it. **And never forget that the initial sales aren't the end goal anyway. Your ultimate goal is to acquire customers that you can build a profitable relationship with.** The profit comes from the *subsequent* sales you make to them, because it's easier to reach out to them and get them to buy. They already like and trust you by then, assuming you've treated them right and delivered a "Wow" experience.

This is a game, and the best marketers win. The best marketers are usually those who are willing to do more than other people, and part of that comes from spending more money than other people spend and being more aggressive with their marketing. **The best marketers take chances, putting themselves out there more; and that's *not* a cost of doing business.** As I said, it's an investment for its future profits, because the real secret is to get people to come back again and again.

In order to do that, of course, you've got to have total integrity. If somebody gets cheated, ripped off, or abused once, they're not likely to come back again. So this requires a commitment on your part to provide superior customer service, and continue to give people what they want the most, and keep being extremely aggressive with your marketing... which all costs money.

So get your mind wrapped around the idea that buying your customers is an investment towards future profits, not a cost. That's what any good marketing strategy is: not a cost, but an investment.

CHAPTER FIVE

QUANTITY LEADS TO QUALITY.

The secret to coming up with the greatest ideas is to come up with lots of ideas! Go wild! Don't hold back! Just get into the habit of letting it flow! Set a time every morning for brainstorming as many ideas as you can come up with, make it fun and enjoyable to crank out huge quantities of ideas — *and you'll be amazed at the little gems that come out of this process!*

Quantity Leads to Quality

The secret to coming up with the greatest ideas is to come up with a lot of ideas. It's as simple as that: you've got to go wild. Don't hold back: throw the filters wide open. **Let *all* the ideas flow in. Set aside some time each day when you're the most productive, and start brainstorming.**

I've talked about this before, in reference to the 5 AM Club, which can actually occur at any time of the day for you. We all have these periods, and for me it's very early in the morning, after those first few cups of coffee. Or sometimes I'll just sit in the shower until I come up with good ideas. We all have a time when we're most creative, so set aside a period during that time to write down all your ideas. **See how many you can come up with, and get them down on paper. The more ideas you come up with, the more *good* ideas you'll come up with.** Some of those will be especially good ideas, or will seem so at the time. Those are the ones that you have to test.

And in that vein, here's a danger that I want to warn you about. A lot of newcomers see these successful entrepreneurial marketing experts, and assume that they're somehow different than the rest of us. They think the experts are superhuman, because they come up with all these good ideas, and everything they touch turns to gold. Well, no. **These people are just the ones who put this method into play full force.**

THE 2-STEP MARKETING SECRET THAT NEVER FAILS!

They come up with a lot of different ideas, they make millions of dollars with the best ones, and then other people become intimidated. They think to themselves, "Man, I could never be that creative. I could never be that smart." I want to dispel that myth right here and now! **My goal here is to convince you that you *do* have the ability to come up with as many multimillion dollar ideas as you want, just like they do, because it's true.**

First of all, like I said, you have to work at it. **You have to set aside a period of time every day when you're just letting those ideas flow without constraint, no matter how unlikely you think some of them are.** Record them as they come to you. I use stacks of legal pads and journals to track my ideas. When Chris Lakey and I are developing ideas together, sometimes he'll pop open a computer file, and as we brainstorm, he'll make a list of all the ideas. **It's like accumulating little pieces of a jigsaw puzzle.** We don't know, in most cases, how these ideas that we come up with are going to be implemented, or if they ever will be; and right then, we don't care. We don't let it bother us.

Many times, the reason why people don't come up with enough good ideas is because they're trying to figure things out too fast. They want everything to appear in their heads full-blown and ready to implement. That happens sometimes, but it's very rare. **By and large, you have to let your ideas develop, grow, and expand.** Just come up with ideas. Write them down. You can figure out later how you're going to implement them. Keep journals, keep notes, keep files in your computer. **Refer back to them constantly. The more you come up with, the better.** And sure, the process may be a little frustrating, and that's one of the reasons why people don't do enough of it. They get frustrated, they get confused, and then they give up. **But you can't give up!**

I'm working on two different product fulfillment projects, and last night I was very confused. I sometimes I like to write notes to myself at night, so that when I'm asleep, part of my brain can be working on the problem. So last night, I started just writing ideas down, knowing that I might figure something out while I slept. This may sound strange to you, but a lot of creative people do that, and it's just one way to be creative. **And this morning, I did in fact wake up with a couple of ideas that I didn't have before I went to bed last night.** I expressed those ideas to Chris on the phone a few hours ago, and sure enough, he and I began brainstorming.

Together, we came up with the ultimate solution. By this time tomorrow, we'll have it all put together. But so many times, people get confused, and they pull back. **They let the pain of the frustration keep them from moving forward, or they try to move forward too fast, trying to figure everything out at once, and they just don't give themselves enough of a break.** You should keep a lot of different projects on your plate and pace yourself, but push yourself. And just let the ideas develop as you go. I've used the driving at night metaphor before. Even if you have to drive 100 miles on the blackest night, all you have to do is be able to see ahead as little as 50 or 100 yards, depending on the conditions. That's enough to get where you need to go, as long as you don't overdrive your headlights. It's the same when it comes to implementing all these ideas that you come up with when you're being creative. You figure things out as you go. You never try to do too much too fast; you just focus on the road ahead.

And mastermind with many others you can; your creativity doesn't need to happen in a vacuum, and really, it shouldn't. No man or woman is an island. I think that working with other people, both within your business and outside it with joint venture partners, is a blessing. It lets you constantly bounce ideas off them. **So brainstorm with your colleagues, and review successful sales material that others are using—both from your allies and your competitors, whether direct or indirect. Combine it with things you've done in the past, and see if you can't cross-fertilize some new concepts.**

Now, I know that this won't work for a lot of people, but here's something I do. I have a 15,000 square foot metal building out here on our property. I can do what I want with it; it's the ultimate "man cave," so to speak. So on the walls of this huge building are all these sales letters we've done in the past, along with some stuff that others have done, and some notes to myself that I've written just to try to stay focused. Some mornings, I'll just do laps in the building, looking at the walls and taking all these things in, subjecting myself to all these different creative ideas.

Again, it's like a jigsaw puzzle. **You put it together a piece at a time, working from what you already know.** Consider a puzzle: it's very confusing to just take 10,000 pieces and throw them down on the ground, and then pick up a few of them and try to put together a coherent image immediately. Different people do puzzles in different ways, but most people like to do the edges first; or they'll try to put a picture within that puzzle. However you do it, you figure it out a little at a time. **The same is true with marketing.** So please don't be intimidated by all these super-creative people who keep coming up with multimillion-dollar ideas. They're working hard at it... and creativity *is* work. Whoever may have told you otherwise is simply wrong. Yes, it can be fun, it's like a game or a jigsaw puzzle in that it's also work. It takes significant time and effort.

Don't try to figure out too much too fast. **Just go at it steadily. Pace yourself but push yourself, figuring it out as you go.** When you feel yourself getting too frustrated, just pull back a little bit. You don't have to let that frustration stop you; just slow down a little. I feel that many people are driven to find that one huge success, and this is particularly frustrating to them. They feel that all the problems they experience, all the monetary woes they have, all their financial problems, would be solved if just *one thing* would click. They need to be that overnight success story; they keep telling themselves, "I'm just one good sales letter away from a million dollars." **And while that's true, you don't get that overnight success by doing something just once and hoping it works.** That's too simplistic and childish, and demonstrates a poor understanding of how the world works. **That's forgetting this secret here: that it's really quantity that leads to quality.**

It's the massive action you take that leads to your success, not just the one thing you do. It's the *many* things you do. It's the cumulative effect of all of the actions, and all of the learning you do, and the life experience that you acquire. I think that's really the secret within the secret here. **The greatest ideas come when you have a lot of ideas, and a lot of ideas**

comes from a lifetime of learning. That doesn't mean that you're constantly studying business, and it doesn't mean that you have a college degree. It's not book learning; **it's life experience, and a dedication to what you're doing.** Consider a musician who learns to play guitar at a young age, and he likes playing guitar, so he does it all the time. At first it sounds horrible, and his parents make him go in the bedroom with the headphones on. They don't want to hear it at all; it's just a lot of noise. Chris Lakey used to play the saxophone when he was a kid, and his parents always got annoyed with the noise. A sax, like any of those instruments that use a reed, can get really squawky, making horrible noises when you're learning. It's really pathetic. And yet, the saxophone is a beautiful instrument, and makes beautiful sounds when played correctly.

I would imagine a guitar player also sounds pretty awful when just getting started. Then they get a few chords under their belt, and after they've got a few years of practice they sound pretty good. They're still not great; but if they keep at it, keep putting in their time and practicing, they may start to be able to play really well and write their own music. What goes into the music they write? It's not just the fact that they know how to play guitar that makes them write good songs. **It's the fact that they have life experience.** By then they may be in their twenties, so they've lived some life. Not as much as some of us, but they've got some experiences, relationships they've had, that they can write about. That makes them a better songwriter and musician. It's not just the fact that they've learned to play, it's all the experiences that they've acquired up to that point.

It's like that in business, too. I think that an

entrepreneur has to learn the basics of their trade, but they also have to accumulate life experiences. They have to commit to being an educated member of society. All my interests and the things I pay the most attention to come out in my writing style and the references I use. **The cumulative effect of your lifetime of experiences makes you a better storyteller, or musician, or performer, or copywriter — whatever it is that you focus on.** This is especially true of older people who have a lifetime of stories and experiences to draw upon. Those become a part of who they are, and in business, they can be useful for many reasons.

In this book, I use a lot of quotes and stories. I've got a good reason for that: there's a lot of life experience there, even outside of specific business strategies. It's one thing to say, "Here's how you do something: A, B, C, D." It's another thing to say, "I read a story about this entrepreneur who did this thing this way. Oh, by the way, the other day I was reading a biography about this other great entrepreneur, and one of the things that they mentioned was *this*." **It's important to be able to pull in those experiences — not just yours, but those of other relevant people — and that's part of what we're talking about here when we talk about quantity.** We're talking about the sum total of everything you do in life, not just business, that becomes a part of your story — a part of who you are.

And then, when you talk about business and specifically about the things you do to make money, not only can you present the things that you've specifically learned about your craft, you can pull in all those other experiences you've encountered while working your business and from life in

general. Chris was telling me today about an article he read this past weekend, about a member of one band from about 20 years ago accusing another band of stealing one of their songs—not the lyrics, but the tune. And the person who wrote the article pointed out that it's completely possible that what had happened was *not* a direct effort to plagiarize, but that this other band had just heard and internalized the tune unconsciously. The shared a record label, so it's possible that the second band heard a demo tape or a concert or something where the first band was demoing this new song—and it influenced them. So several years later, when the second band was laying down their own music for a new song they were writing, that memory was tapped and made use of on a subconscious level. Apparently, this is quite common. They didn't intentionally plagiarize, but the memory of that tune was in their heads; so when it came time for them to write the tune for this new song they were working on, that familiar tune just came out and seemed to write itself. So they ended up with a new song that sounded similar, with similar riffs, chords, tones, and cadences. It wasn't deliberate; it was just a subconscious memory the songwriter drew on.

I think a copywriter can do the same thing, if they're not careful. Even if you have no intention of actually plagiarizing someone else's work, just the fact that you keep a swipe file so that you can study your competitors' sales material might generate some unintentional similarities. You spend a lot of time researching, dedicating yourself to the craft of being a better copywriter by studying what other people are doing in the marketplace... then, at some point down the road, you're writing a new sales letter or you're designing an ad, and you subconsciously draw upon an idea that you saw someone else use. It could be an idea for a headline. It could just be the way you're designing a postcard or an entire sales letter. **The point is, something you've internalized may subconsciously become the basis of something new you've created.**

Your experience as a copywriter, which comes partly from studying copy that other people do, becomes the basis of anything you write. **So while you do have to carefully consider whether what you've created may owe too much to someone else's creation, the concept here is that the more you have to draw on, the more you'll be able to pull from.** And you never really know when something's going to become useful in the future: when there's going to be a story to draw from, or an experience that may serve you five or ten years down the road. **By absorbing life and all the experiences that life has to offer, you allow those experiences to become a part of your story, part of who you are.**

This contributes to the quantity and quality of the ideas you have. All those things can flow together, with the end result that they produce better ideas, because you've had more ideas. I've talked before about photographers, and how one of the main things that separates a good photographer from an average one is the number of pictures they take. Although they do sometimes have an eye for their photography or for just getting the right set up or angle, a lot of it's the result of taking massive action, getting a ton of pictures, and then finding some good ones in there.

If you only take one picture, there's a good chance something could go wrong. Someone might blink or look away from the camera. But if you take a hundred pictures of that same pose, hopefully one is going to be the right one. That quantity leads to finding the quality, and that's the strategy here. **So, massive action and massive life experience leads to the quality that can produce the results you're looking for. More leads to more.** You have to test a lot of ideas, and through the process of testing you find out what works the best.

I hope you're convinced now that you can definitely be one of those people that comes up with multimillion-dollar ideas by simply coming up with a lot of ideas, by being very free with your brainstorming and testing a lot of different things. **I think you need to be very open about it, too.** Some people are so secretive; they'd rather keep it all close to their vests. That's nonsense. **Implementation is so difficult that you can give people your best ideas constantly, and rarely have to worry about anybody stealing them.**

CHAPTER SIX

The art of being wise is the art of knowing what to overlook.

➤ Fight for focus!

➤ Spend the majority of your time on the few projects that can bring you the largest amount of sales and profits.

➤ Ignore the advice from those around you who do not understand the big picture!

➤ Prioritize!

Know What to Overlook

In full, it goes like this: **"The art of being wise is the art of knowing what to overlook."** Often, you have to fight for focus. **You have to prioritize, spending the majority of your time on those projects that can bring in the most sales and profits, ignoring advice from all the people around you who don't understand the bigger picture.** Now, I've talked a little about how it helps to surround yourself with people you can brainstorm with. But if the people around you don't have a clue about how your business works and what's most important to you, then you don't want to be looking to them for any kind of advice.

Let me share a little story with you. When my wife, Eileen, and I first got started back in 1988, we combined a couple of ideas that were working for other people, and presented them to the marketplace in a new and different way. Soon we were making about $500 a day. Then we met Russ von Hoelscher; and **because he had 20 years of experience and we did everything he told us to, we went on to achieve enormous success, making $10 million in our first five years in business.**

One of the things that used to just drive me crazy was when I would give Russ one of my best ideas and he would very quickly say, "Oh, that idea won't work." But now that I've got over 20 years of experience myself, I find myself doing it again and again with others. **See, I know what works and what**

doesn't now. That's not to say that you shouldn't test new ideas, but you do have to be able to prioritize—and by prioritizing, I mean that you have to know what works best and spend the majority of your time on those things, while also testing some newer ideas that may eventually work better still. That's one way to do it. **Take those few things that you know work the best and expand on them.** If you don't have enough experience to do that, then look for commonalities, common denominators used by your competitors over and over again. Those will tell you what you need to be doing. **Then find ways to modify what they're doing, ways to do it all better, and apply them to your own product line.**

Whether you're drawing on your previous successes or other people's successes for inspiration, beneath the surface you're still working with those same proven ideas, **so you don't need to reinvent the wheel.**

This is the one secret that we've used repeatedly over the years that's been worth more money than just about any secret I could share. **We're constantly creating new stuff, over and over. Why do we do it? Because that's what our clients want.** They're addicted to anything that's new... and it's not just our clients. The whole world is addicted to new stuff. People have shorter attention spans than ever before; they're after the shiny new object in the distance. **But the thing is, if it's too new, then that novelty could backfire.** It may get their attention for a little while, but they'll quickly become skeptical.

So you really have to prioritize your ideas by knowing what's most important to your clientele, and overlooking the rest. What do they want the very most? What are the general themes that keep working again and again in your market? Once you've identified and adopted those, you have to find new ways to make things look a little different on the surface, while maintaining all those things that you know they want the most.

If that's just a little too conceptual for you, then let me give you a couple of fast examples. Consider Procter & Gamble. This is a multibillion dollar company; you walk down the grocery store aisles, and you see all these Proctor & Gamble products — and they always seem to be new and improved. They're *always* doing something new. The more you look for this, the more you'll see it. **Really, it's the same soap powder or pills or whatever the case may be; but there's always something new about it, isn't there?**

Another quick example: popular music bands. I'm most familiar with rock music, but country does it too; I've listened to enough country to know that, just like rock, it's the same basic song over and over again. **They do a few things to make it sound a bit different, but underneath it's basically the same.** And look at cars. Every four or five years, maybe, they'll introduce a major design change; but it's never huge. Even as we record this, the brand new Mustangs look more or less like the original Mustangs did back in '64. There are some differences, but they still have that same basic design. **That's because that's what the market wants.** Although we're creating things that are new, new, new, because our customers are addicted to new, they still want things to be the same underneath. **Our job as marketers is to is give them more of what they want, which is a lot easier to do if we've prioritized enough first, using this secret.**

THE 2-STEP MARKETING SECRET THAT NEVER FAILS!

We know what produces the most sales and profit, the things that they want the most. And then we just keep finding ways to make things appear to be new on the surface, maintaining enough of what we know they want underneath, so they'll keep buying again and again. That's how we ensure that they'll be attracted to whatever it is we offer. **It has a little of the new, a little of the old.** There are some very famous marketers whom we've spoken to over the years, who've gotten on our customer list and seen what we've done. They've said to us, "How in the world do you keep creating all this new stuff?" Well, I just explained the process to you. That's precisely how we do it.

There's a classic business concept that simply says, "Work *on* your business, not *in* it." I understand that very well, at a deeply personal level. When my wife stepped down as the president and CEO of M.O.R.E., Inc. in 2001, I took over. Let me tell you, it was the worst two and a half years of my life! I'd go over to the office and I'd spend my whole day putting out brush fires. I'd come home exhausted; and although I'd worked my ass off all day and was damned tired, I couldn't name three or four things that I'd really accomplished. **I was just putting out all these little brushfires all day long—taking care of small crises that other people could and should have handled.** I was working *in* the business, not on it.

By working on it and not in it, you're able stand back. You're able to focus a little: you can spend more of your time on the fewer things that make you the most money, while delegating the rest of it to others. It's just a good business principle. Remember, the most successful people in the world all have those same 168 hours that you have every week. They've just found ways to prioritize, so that they're able to get the most leverage they can in the time that they have. This is one method of enforcing that concept. It lets you pick your battles—something many of us learn as kids, while others don't pick up on it until adulthood, if ever. There are times when you just want to let something go, because there are more important things to worry about. **The minor things pale to significance when you focus on what really matters.**

So let the little stuff go in favor of the big things. By doing this, you prioritize by necessity, and end up spending your energy worrying about things that actually matter. Chris Lakey tells me that he would probably tell his three-year-old "No" more often than he does, if he was one of those parents who worried about every little thing a kid does. Inevitably, the kid does a lot to annoy him, and there are times that Chris wants to tell him "No" because it would just be an inconvenience to say "Yes." But Chris has learned to pick his battles with his son. He has to decide that if it's not going to hurt the child, then it probably *is* okay to say "Yes," even though Chris might not want to get up and do something for him or with him at that moment.

That strategy of picking your battles means that you let some stuff go, and you only worry about the really important things. **That's what we're talking about here, with the wisdom to overlook.** What few items can bring you the biggest return on your investment? Which projects should be overlooked until you have time to work on them, if you ever do? And by the way, don't ever let people fool you into thinking that your time isn't an investment. Time is money, unless of course it's spent willingly. There's nothing wrong with a vacation, or in deciding not to do something for a while. Sometimes you've got to decide to go to the beach, or that you're going to go spend time with family. You're not intentionally avoiding work; you're resting. **Otherwise, when you're working on some facet of your business, time *is* money.** The time you invest in your business is either time well spent or it's time wasted, depending on what you're doing. **So you've got to prioritize.**

You prioritize by determining what really matters to your market, and how you can most profitably provide those things. It's as simple (and as difficult) as that. Get advice if you must, but again, ignore advice from people who don't understand the big picture. I understand the influence that friends and family have in your life, but the truth is, most of them are worried that you'll fail—so they give you advice that assumes that you can't succeed in the first place. **We see this all the time. In many cases, our clients are not full-time business people; though we do have some customers who are already financially successful, looking to expand their portfolios, most are involved in small or home-based businesses.** They're either working part-time and hoping to eventually quit their regular jobs, or they're looking to supplement their retirement income somehow.

As such, most of our clients are hearing from people all the time, mostly getting negative advice: "Don't do this. Don't do that. Avoid this. Avoid that." Quite often they tell us, "You know, my family members are telling me I shouldn't get into business. I shouldn't waste my time trying to make money. I shouldn't try to better my life. I should just accept where I'm at, work for somebody else, and give up the dream." This is ironic, because the people who are giving them this advice are, in most cases, just as bad off as they are. **They've never tried to better themselves, so how can they know?** They're stuck in jobs they hate, they can't make money for themselves, and they've got no business experience and certainly no track record of success.

And yet they're trying to tell other people how to live their lives, and how to run their businesses. When we talk about ignoring people around you who don't understand the big picture, that's exactly the kind of thing we're talking about. If you're going to be in business for yourself, and you want to get into a certain business, **don't ask for or listen to advice from people who are broke, especially if they've never run a business themselves.** Talk to people who have been in business, who have run successful businesses, and get *them* to give you advice on what you should and shouldn't do.

That's one of the things you have to consider when it comes to focusing on the most important things. **People who don't know what they're talking about should be overlooked, simple as that.** You're going to have all kinds of people bending your ear with advice, so a big step toward your success will be knowing who to pay attention to, and who to avoid.

And besides whether or not you should listen to individual people, part of the process is also evaluating opportunities as they come to you. **You need to be able to choose a few important things to focus your time and energy on.** As you evaluate opportunities, especially when you're struggling, it's easy to feel like you need to pursue *every* opportunity... but that's desperation talking. If you take a chance on everything, you're going to dilute your chances of succeeding. **If you think that everything is an opportunity worth pursuing, you're going to miss out, because you're unfocused.** Don't take the attitude that you have to take massive action on everything, just because you need something to work. You still need to stick with your game plan. You still need to evaluate opportunities, and make good, sound decisions. **Be willing and able to overlook some things, and focus on the most important things. That will put you in a better position to capitalize on all the opportunities you participate in.**

And it helps to have a good strategy, too, something that keeps you running towards your goals. Right now, Chris Lakey and I are working on such a strategy. Chris came up with the idea of letting our clients take care of a major portion of our marketing expenditure on a weekly basis. We give them a tremendous opportunity at the same time, though, so they don't mind doing that. Once Chris convinced us that this was a doable strategy, it became our main priority. Now, we're focused on it. We're developing all kinds of new ideas that we would never have spent as much time, work, and effort creating otherwise. And of course, it includes a lot of our existing stuff; because remember, you've got to stick with those themes that you know people want the most. **Yet a major part of our resources is being put into the new elements of this new strategy, because we see that this is something that can give us a tremendous advantage in the future, and help our clients at the same time.** So it's a win/win situation.

By maintaining a good strategy, you're able to be like

those horses wearing blinders. You've probably seen pictures of such horses, or maybe you've seen them in parades. Blinders are little shields on the outsides of their eyes, which allow the horses to focus on what's ahead without distraction. They can't see things to the left or right at all because of the blinders. Now, I've also seen pictures where they take a little carrot and dangle it in front of the horse. The horse will keep moving because they see that carrot there, never realizing that the carrot is on a string, attached to its head.

That may not be the best analogy here, but the point is that you have to stay focused on what's ahead. **You've got to fight for your focus, and you've got to know what to focus on. Everything else has to be overlooked.**

CHAPTER SEVEN

There's a lot of competition for your customers' money. <u>Never forget</u> <u>this</u>. If you can't answer the question: "Why should I give it to *you* and not *your competitor*?" then you don't deserve to be in business.

Just like in sports; the team who wants it more than the other team — wins!

Never Forget the Competition!

There's a lot of competition for your customer's money. Never forget this! There are plenty of other people out there trying to attract the same customers *you're* trying to attract. **If you can't answer the customer's question, "Why should I give my money to you and not your competitor?" then you just don't deserve to be in business.** That may sound tough, even ruthless, but you have to be ruthless to succeed in business. So you can never forget this question. You've got to burn it into your head—and then you've got to find logical, beneficial ways to answer it. **You start by learning to think like your customer.**

Consider sports teams. All other things being equal, the teams that consistently win are the ones that most *want* to win. **Let's face it: in a nutshell, the market is overcrowded.** There are more competitors than ever before, because the barriers of entry into business are becoming lower and lower. **This means it's harder for anyone who gets into the business to succeed, since the consumer has many more choices now.**

One thing that this has led to is a fragmentation of the market. **Not only are there more niche markets than ever, but there are niches within the niches, because customers can demand to have things exactly the way they want them.** And they *are* more demanding: there used to be a saying that "the customer is the king," but now it's more accurate to say that the customer is a child dictator. They're like a fat little kid who demands and gets everything he wants, so he's spoiled rotten. That's who the average consumer is these days. That's who you have to please and appease in your market.

Because consumers only have so much disposable income and have more choices than ever before, they can afford to be very choosy. This has led to some evolutionary pressure among the marketers in their niches. Some of these marketers are getting laser sharp, more so all the time; they're becoming very, very good at what they do. **The upshot of this is that you have to fight for your customer's money. To make the profits you need in order to succeed, you have to be aggressive.**

You can't run from these problems when it comes to asking people to give you their money, because people are extremely selfish. They may be generous in other areas of their life, but when it comes to giving up money they're not generous at all. For the most part, they're also very selfish and apathetic, and quite aware that market crowding provides them with plenty of options to chose some. Add in the hype, where everybody's trying to scream louder than the next guy, and the customers become incredibly cynical and jaded. That's part of what drives their apathy: they don't believe what anyone says anymore, given all the hyperbole and, often, the outright lying.

So on the one hand they're like little dictators, who want more and more; in fact, the more you give them, the more they want. They're not grateful for anything—they're just demanding. On the other hand, they think they've heard it all, so they don't believe anything anymore; this makes them very selfish when it comes to giving anyone their money. **They're all** wondering, **"What's in it for me? Why should I choose you?" That means that you have to create offers that are better than those that your competitors create.** And I'm not just talking about your direct competitors: there's a lot of indirect competition too. There are plenty of other products unrelated to your market that your customers can spend their disposable income on.

To get their attention, then, you have to create irresistible offers that go way over the top... **and you must realize that as time passes, it takes more and more to get people's attention. That's a sad reality of life; so you either have to accept it and deal with it, or get out of the game.** Because this is a trend that isn't going away; in fact, it's only going to grow. Your consumers are going to become more jaded, more skeptical, more apathetic, more resistant to every sales message out there. The competitors who survive this winnowing process are going to get smarter and smarter.

Now, I'm not saying all this to be negative at all—in fact, I don't see it as a negative thing. You've got to rise to the challenge! **You've got to be aggressive, you've got to stay hungry, you've got to fight!** You've got to win those customers over; you've got to fight for their business. **You've got to give them all kinds of compelling reasons to buy from you: reasons that are so compelling, in fact, they have no *choice* but to do business with you.** You've got to keep coming up with offers that are so good that people just can't ignore them, can't refuse them, can't *not* order.

Competition is important to keep in mind; but in another sense, we try not to focus on it too much, because all

you can really control is what *you* do. Here at M.O.R.E., Inc. we believe that your best defense against competition is a good offense: to just do your job right, being as aggressive in your marketing as possible, not worrying too much about your competition. Even though there *is* a lot of competition for your customers' money and you have to keep that in mind, you can't focus on that exclusively, or you'll lose sight of your own objectives. **If instead you focus on being the best marketer that you can be, you'll always be head and shoulders above your competition, because most of them aren't worried about that.** They're not thinking about it from that perspective.

That doesn't mean you should ever lose sight of that question I asked at the beginning of this chapter, the one that's every-present in the prospect's mind: "Why should I give my money to you and not your competitor?" What's your answer to that question? **If you can't tell your prospect why they should choose you over your competition, then they're probably going to choose your competition.** It doesn't matter whether that competition is direct or indirect; in fact, I think it's foolish to forget that they can spend their money outside your marketplace if they want to.

Ultimately, a prospect in your marketplace really has three options. They can do business with you, they can do business with one of your competitors, or they can do business with neither of you. They'll still spend their money; it will just be spent somewhere else. **The fact is, we're competing not just within our marketplace but with all other marketplaces.** If someone happens to have a $100 left after they pay their bills, they're going to have to decide what to do with that $100.

They're seeing your offers, they're seeing your competitors' offers, and they're also seeing McDonald's offers. You might not think of McDonald's as a competitor, unless you're Burger King; but if they eat at McDonald's instead of spending that money on you, McDonald's does become your competitor— albeit an indirect competitor. After eating at McDonald's a few times, they're not going to have much of that $100 left to buy whatever it is you're selling.

So that's a big factor here. **You're fighting against all the other things that take their money, whether those are direct competitors or not.** So how do you fight their urge to spend at other places? Again, by finding out what they want the most, so that you can make them want to spend that money with *you* instead of with anybody else. What makes you stand out from everybody else they could do business with?

Here at M.O.R.E., Inc., we're in the process of creating a brand new offer that we feel will help people in our marketplace sell just about any product or service. One of the challenges in our marketplace is that there are a lot of people who are involved in selling various network marketing, affiliate or distributor opportunities. **Inevitably, large groups of people end up selling the same products and services.** When this is the case, it becomes difficult to distinguish yourself in the marketplace. You end up making the same offer that 100 or 1,000 other distributors or affiliates are already making, so why would someone want to buy from you?

Well, we've put together a package that's worth over $13,000, consisting of 180 of our best money-making products and programs, that distributors can give away as a

free gift. By doing this, we're helping clients distinguish themselves in the marketplace by saying, "Hey! Not only can you buy this product or service that you can get from any other distributor, but when you buy from us, we're going to add on this free gift—this fantastic bonus of 180 money-making programs worth over $13,000! You're going to get it free! Nobody else has the rights to give this super bonus package away, but you can get it from us."

This will help people separate themselves from all the competition selling the same products or services. That's one of the ways we're helping our clients distinguish themselves. No matter what marketplace you're in, you've got to do *something* to separate yourself from the crowd. **So what do you offer that they can't get from your competitors?** Maybe it's a special gift, like the one I've just mentioned. Maybe it's an added service, some feature or benefit that they can't get from someone else. Maybe you deliver to their doorstep, and nobody else in your marketplace does. Maybe you have an extra service you provide on top of what they would normally buy. There are all kinds of things you can do. **You just have to pick which ones that you think are going to be the most valuable to your marketplace.**

Again, the best thing to do is ask yourself what they really want the most, what they want really *bad*, and what you, specifically, can give them that they can't get from anyone else. This is critical, because you have to remember that as they're deciding whether they want to do business with you, they're asking themselves, **"What's in it for me?"** Everybody in your marketplace wants to know what you're doing for them.

What do you bring to the table in this relationship? They're telling you, whether tacitly or explicitly, "You're asking for my money, and I'm deciding whether or not to give it to you. A big part of whether I say "yes" will be determined by how much I believe you're going to give me in this relationship, and what I'm going to get out of doing business with you." **If you can answer the question "What's in it for me?" adequately, and make a compelling enough case, they'll choose to do business with you.**

I think the main thing to take out of this is that there are so many different ways that people choose to spend their money. Therefore, don't worry just about your direct competitors when you're thinking about the competition. Add in all those other things people can do with their money. **And keep this in mind: almost everyone has a certain level of discretionary income, no matter what marketplace they're in, and in almost every case, they're going to spend it.** Very few people will save it; the national savings average is virtually nothing. Either people are drowning in debt, or they're saving very, very little. Most people live paycheck to paycheck. Most people aren't even saving for retirement, or they're doing a very poor job of it. They've got their fixed bills, they've got all the things they're normally spending money on, and then they've got their discretionary income that brings them down to zero until the next paycheck. And some people are living on credit cards beyond their means.

All that money is going out into the marketplace. It's going to McDonald's. It's going to the clothing store for T-shirts, or sneakers, or whatever the latest fashion item may be. It's going to the movie theater and Wal-Mart. It's going toward the latest high-definition television, or the latest gadget or gizmo. Some is even going into your marketplace, to buy the kinds of products and services you sell. **But there's only so much money, and they're spending it all every month, so you've got to make a compelling case for why they should spend it on *you*.** Give them a reason to do business with you, and not your competition. If you'll do that consistently, with an aggressive marketing strategy, you'll find yourself getting a bigger market share. **You'll find yourself winning out over your competition, over and over again.**

To maximize your possibility for success, you should look for markets where most of the members are insatiable. The hungrier they are for whatever it is that you're selling, the more they can't get enough of it, the more you can profit— because they just keep coming back for more. **Focus on those markets and build your business around them.** That will give you a real competitive advantage, much more so than if you're dealing with other markets where people don't have that insatiability factor built in.

I'll never forget one of the most important lessons I've ever learned. One of our vice presidents, Randy Hamilton, has been with our company almost since the very beginning. He's an accountant/bookkeeper, and when he first started working with us, he took a look at the products we were selling and he thought, "Oh, man, I've *got* to get another job. There's no way this company is going to make it long-term." Remember, we weren't even a year old at the time.

Then he forgot about it. We had plenty of work, and he just got buried in it. A couple of months later, he told himself, "Man,

82

I've got to get my resume out there. I've *got* to update my resume. I've got to get another job. This company isn't going to make it." And, well, he kept saying that to himself for years. Every once in a while, he would remind himself this company wasn't going to make it long term... and it's been 23 years now. Eventually he forgot it. Now, Randy is a real smart guy: He's got an IQ off the charts. But at the very beginning, he definitely didn't understand the market we're serving. **You see, we sell business opportunities to people who are insatiable in their desire to find the right business opportunity.** They just keep buying and buying. Thank God they do. Randy just didn't know that... and his experience has taught me one of the most important lessons I've ever learned. And here it is: **if you get involved in the right market, you don't ever have to worry.** Half the battle is already won. So pick your market very, very carefully. And never forget that there are many other people trying to get your customer's money.

Another way we work around that problem is by using direct mail, which I've championed many times already in this book. It's our main marketing method, and we prefer it to everything else. And yet, we realize that when we send out a direct mail letter, it's not just showing up in our customer's mailbox all by itself. It's showing up with a bunch of other direct mail postcards and packages from our competitors, because our customers are also on the mailing lists of our competitors. In the course of a week, they may get 20-30 pieces of mail along with the little direct mail letter that we spent so much time working on. **Our letter is competing with all the other stuff in their mailbox — and the more we're aware of that, the stronger our offers become.**

THE 2-STEP MARKETING SECRET THAT NEVER FAILS!

Now, the problems I've discussed here aren't an attempt to discourage you in your marketing efforts; quite the opposite. Let yourself be empowered by all this. Look: it's a game, it's a hunt. The fiercest competitors are always the ones who win, so you've got to be aggressive. You've got to stay hungry. **You've got to create irresistible offers, and you have to keep finding ways to do things to differentiate yourself, so you stand out in the marketplace.** You're different, so you have to think differently, and you have to think aggressively. Don't become overwhelmed by this. Look at it as the ultimate challenge, one that tests your ability to rise above it all and overcome all those competitors—direct and indirect—trying to take that income that could and should be yours.

CHAPTER EIGHT

You can <u>never</u> know the true value of something until and unless you compare it with something else.

◆

This is a powerful marketing strategy that you <u>must</u> incorporate into <u>all</u> of your sales material. Find as many ways as possible to associate yourself, your company, and your products and services with other items that have the greatest value in the minds and hearts of the people in your market.

Determining True Value

You can never know the true value of something until and unless you compare it with something else. This is a powerful marketing strategy that you've got to incorporate into *all* of your sales material. **You've got to find as many ways as possible to associate yourself, your company, your products and your services with other items that have great value in the minds and hearts of your prospects.** Unlike so many of the 500 Ways, which are based on common sense more than anything else, this is a genuine secret: it's not something, by and large, that a study of the marketplace is going to easily reveal.

In this section, I'm going to outline a number of ways to help you understand how to incorporate this secret into your money-making process.

First of all, never compare apples to apples. You always need to compare apples to oranges; and when I say apples to oranges, **I'm talking about you helping people understand the value of your product or service by comparing it with something of a much higher value.** When we first started selling $5,000 seminars, all our sales materials compared the cost of a traditional business to what we were offering: a complete, turnkey business opportunity for just $5000. **When we showed them what a traditional business would cost to start up, it made the price of our opportunity seem small by comparison. So we were comparing apples to oranges, and that's just one example of how to do this.

When you create the sales material, you have to do the thinking for the people you intend to read it—and not because they're stupid. It has nothing to do with mental capacity at all. It has to do with the way people read sales material. They look everything over in a skeptical, apathetic, even cynical kind of way. **And unless you're doing the comparisons for them, they're never going to really think things through; they don't have the time or energy.** So again, you've got to think things through for them. For an example, on our advertising and management service, one position usually costs less than a dollar a day. And so what we have is a little comparison table that shows what you can buy for a dollar. We give you 30-35 different comparisons of what you normally pay a dollar for, to try to get you to think the way we think, which is this: that a dollar is nothing. You can spend a dollar a day without even thinking about it. People are constantly spending a buck here, a buck there, and not even giving it a second thought. **So we give you many different examples of things that you commonly buy for a dollar that you don't even think about.** We're making those comparisons for people, helping them think it though.

We also do a thorough job of educating customers. For example, we have a product that shows you how to turn 33 cents a day into thousands of dollars a month. **In the literature for that product, we offer 27 different examples of problems faced by various businesses, and then we show you how our opportunity solves each one of those problems.** We're helping people understand the value of what we have by comparing it with something else. **That's the *only* way you know something is valuable: by having something to compare it with.** And you have to make those comparisons to your prospective buyers in a clear, forceful way, to educate them on why what you have to offer is worth every penny that you say it is. **You can't expect them to figure it out on their own.**

Another example: we have something called our Club-20 International opportunity, which is a whole different way to make money with multi-level marketing. Now, anybody can make a statement like that. **But in the marketing material, what we've done is carefully describe the four problems that are inherent with all multi-level marketing opportunities, before showing how our compensation plan and opportunities eliminated or were a solution to those problems.** We did a direct, simple comparison for people. We didn't just make some statement without backing it up with examples. **Comparisons are important,** because they help people think through things, by showing them all the different problems and how we solve those problems.

Here's another example. We have a certain kind of website we're developing right now called the ATM website, where ATM stands for Automatic Transporter Method. **But we also tell people that one reason we chose that name, ATM, was that the system works like an ATM cash machine.** These websites are designed to pay people just as if they had their own cash machines. We show a picture of an ATM machine, and we make those comparisons so that people make that connection. People already know what an ATM machine is, so we're comparing our web sites with one. We're showing them how the ATM website can profit them.

You've got to build your case for your product; that's a foundation principle of marketing. You can't just say that you've got the best product or service, because *everybody* does that... and nobody believes it anymore. **So it's up to you to prove that it's true, by giving them specific, dramatic examples.** That's one of the reasons you compare things, one of the reasons you give examples. **You want to *prove* the value of what you've got to people.** That's why we started doing that from the very beginning with our websites. We showed people the prices that they would normally pay for different hosting services, using real companies, so people could see that we weren't just making this stuff up. I've said this before in these pages, and doubtless will again: when people read your sales material, they don't believe a damn word that you say. **Therefore, you've got to prove to them that what you're saying is the honest truth.**

So we put together a program called the Yellow Page Challenge. Basically, we called all these website developers and asked them what their prices were, pretending we were prospective buyers—and we recorded their responses, and just let *them* tell it. We showed people the truth in a dramatic way. **We didn't just say that our websites were worth this much money; we actually proved it, using real-world comparisons.**

Making these kinds of sharp, contrasting comparisons takes people from where they're at to where you want them to be. Most of the time as a marketer, you can be assured that the people reading your sales material are pretty much apathetic. They've seen it all before, and they don't really trust what they've seen. So this is your opportunity as a marketer to be very creative, to take them from where they're at to where you want them to be—and where you want them to be is a paying customer. **Properly handled, these comparisons and contrasts raise the value of your product in the mind of your prospect, so what you're selling them becomes very critical.**

You especially have to build the case that the money they're going to spend with you is paltry—that it's hardly anything compared to the benefits and the value they're going to receive from your product. You see this in a lot of savvy marketing out there. It's unfortunate that this is a lesson that many, many marketers don't understand—this strategy of entering their prospects' minds and thinking along to the point where you want them to get to, where you want them to buy.

This strategy helps you understand exactly what you to have to do to get them there. I have a friend and colleague, Chris Hollinger, who used to be a teacher. He says that back then, he always started from the point of the student knowledge base: that is, he looked first at where the students were, then at where he wanted to take them. What happened in between is the science and the art of teaching. Well, making a sell is no different. You have a prospect who comes to you with their own prejudices, their own pre–conceived notions, and it's your job as the marketer to get them to the final result, which is them saying "yes": "Yes, I want to join your opportunity; Yes, I want your product; Yes, I want your service."

It's these comparisons that relay that. The more selling and copywriting you do, the more *thinking* you do about your particular products, services or opportunities, the better at this you'll become. You'll get so good at making those comparisons that in the end, they're going to say, "Wow, you mean I'm going to get all this for only *this* much money? All these benefits? Wow!" **These comparisons help you get from point A to point B in the selling process.** You're helping them to see what you're seeing, building that value in their mind to a tremendous level, making what you're offering look incredibly worthwhile. **Remember, people don't want cheap things; they want valuable things for cheap prices. Therefore, it's up to us to establish that value, and prove it beyond any doubt they might have.** It seems simple, and really, it *is* simple—and yet most people don't do enough of it. If you're having trouble figuring it out yourself, I'd say study the good marketers and see how they're doing it. Clearly, they're doing a great job of proving to people that what they say is true.

Also, here's an idea: think like a lawyer. **Consider all the possible objections someone could bring up, and address them first.** Either show how they're erroneous, or how your product overcomes them. **Just as a lawyer would, build a strong case based on the preponderance of evidence—not just a little proof.** Go overboard if you must. That's the way you have to be, I think, when you sell things for a living.

CHAPTER NINE

❖❖ ❖❖ ❖❖

Stay very close
to your customer.

Know your customers <u>better</u> than they know themselves. How? By thinking about them all the time and realizing that <u>the</u> <u>real</u> <u>reasons</u> they buy are mostly unconscious.

❖❖ ❖❖ ❖❖

Stay Very Close to Your Customer

Here's a topic we've touched on in a variety of ways elsewhere in this book. Basically, you have to stay very close to your customer, in the sense that you need to know your customers better than they know themselves. How? **By thinking about them all the time, and by realizing that the real reasons they buy are mostly unconscious.** The reasons why most of us buy *anything* are mostly unconscious. Most of our actions are unconscious, in fact. That's just Psychology 101, and good marketing is simply math and psychology. You have to have an intimate understanding of who your customers are, what they want, what they don't want, what they like, and what they don't like. **You've got to think like they think.** If I had to come up with one thing that's made us more money than any other thing, this would be it.

When we first got started, we knew very well who the market was, because we were part of the market. We'd been buying up all these money–making programs for years. We were on all of the mailing lists, and it became very easy for us to know what the opportunity market wanted, because we *were* the opportunity market. It takes one to know one, as a child will often say. We knew who the customers were because the customers were us. That's why one of the things we suggest to a lot of our clients is simply this: bloom where you're planted. Take a page out of our playbook. **The opportunity market is**

made up of millions of people who are just like you. Look in the mirror and point. *You* **are the opportunity market.** If you're looking for a market to get into that you already intimately understand, believe it or not (and I'd like for you to really think about this) you *are* this market.

People buy for emotional reasons. They buy for unconscious reasons. And oftentimes, what people really want are things that are highly irrational. It's up to you to try to figure out why they buy what they buy. And I know it sounds like simple common sense, but you've got to dig deeper and go beyond what's visible on the surface. I mean, for instance, you might say, "People in the opportunity market want to make more money." Of course they do, but it goes way beyond that. **There are many deeply emotional reasons why people buy all these money–making opportunities and biz opps.**

To figure those reasons out, you've got to try to stay close to your customer. One of the reasons why we love doing our live events, where we meet with our clients, is simply that they help us understand our clients better. **You have to think about your customers all the time. Constantly. What do they want?** What are they really looking for, and how can you provide it to them, and how can you serve it up better than anyone else?

Here's an idea I got from one of the greatest copywriters in this country right now — a man who charges tens of thousands of dollars for writing sales letters. **As a creative exercise, ask yourself this question:** *If I had God-like superpowers, and I could give my customers anything that they wanted, what would it be?* And then just start brainstorming, coming up with all kinds of ideas. Some of your ideas may seem a little foolish, but just keep coming up with these ideas, thinking like your customers the whole time. Quantity ultimately leads to quality, as long as you're inside their minds and hearts. And don't choose a market just because you think it's going to make you a lot of money. **Choose a market that you know something about, one that you have an intimate awareness of. If you don't, your ignorance can cost you dearly.**

One thing that separates my work from me having a job, as opposed to something that I choose to do, something that I *enjoy* doing, **is the fact that one of the aspects of my work is to think critically about my marketplace, about my business, and about my customers.** And ironically enough, it's one of the most creative things I do, simply *because* I'm always evaluating how my offer—how my infrastructure, how my marketing, how a particular advertising campaign, how my *entire message*—will play between the ears of my customers. **As a marketer, I'm always dealing with psychology: the wants and needs and desires of my customers. That's basic to the profession.**

And I don't need to tell anybody reading this that people are absolutely crazy in their own ways... and yet we sell to these people. They're our customers: **so being able to think critically and even creatively about your marketplace, about who your customers are and what's going to get their attention, about what's going to get them to act and what they're going to like—that's vitally important.** And often, when you're immersed in a particular industry, as we are, you're right there in the middle of it. You look in the mirror to find your marketplace, because they *are* you.

THE 2-STEP MARKETING SECRET THAT NEVER FAILS!

Even if you think that doesn't apply to you, consider this: you're probably on some kind of mailing list right now. I suspect you're receiving things in the mail constantly: not just from me, but from other marketers as well. **You *are* the home-based business industry, in and of itself.** So take the time to think critically, not just about the nuts and bolts of what you're doing, but about who your customers are. Consider, for example, network marketing, which is where many people in this field get started.

Now, I realize that not everybody has the same knack for selling that I do or Chris Lakey does. There are some people who are just better at it. Yet most network marketing companies out there force you to sell, which may not be something that's normally in your nature. Furthermore, one of the biggest fears most people have is public speaking. You have to train yourself to do that, and some people are just more gifted at it than others. Well, knowing all that tells me that most people are going to need systems to plug into, because they're not going to be able to go out there and sell with standard network marketing tactics right away. They're not going to be that dynamic guy who gets up in front of a group and talks. **So if you're going at it from a networking perspective, what can you do for your customers so they don't have to go out there and be super salesmen, but still make decent money?**

Clearly, you need to develop systems with your customers in mind, so you really have to reflect on the constraints of your marketplace and of the people involved in it. In the network marketing example, people want to make money—but they don't want to have to talk to other people.

Okay, so what can you do to help them make money when 90% of the companies out there are saying you're going to *have* to talk to people, you're going to have to drive people to a conference call, you're going to have to invite them to a conference or ambush them in your homes? If you can build a system that limits or eliminates that need in the right way, then that becomes a very big attractor. **Find a way to tell your prospects, "Look, you can make money with this business and not have to talk to anybody."** That's a big issue right there for the vast majority of home-based business people. That's a winning message. It's been done over and over. We've done it here at M.O.R.E., Inc.

When it comes to thinking like a customer, you just can't work in a vacuum. Study them closely so you can gauge their needs, and especially their wants. **If you study enough successful letters, websites, or sales material of any kind in any market, you'll see the same common denominators continue to show up.** These are clues to what people want, so just add those messages to yours.

There are other ways to do this, too. One of the things I'm so thankful for here at M.O.R.E., Inc. is our sales department. **They're on the phone constantly with our clients, every single day. And thank goodness we get their feedback, because sometimes the customers are thinking totally differently than we think they are!** As an example, we had a program this year that I thought customers would get really excited about... but it turned out that they weren't interested at all. Our sales department helped us determine that more quickly than we might have otherwise. And here's what it was: we were offering to give away up to 10,000 postcards absolutely free to all of our clients. We got all pumped up about it, so we thought the customers were going to just jump up and down at the prospect. But here's the thing: it turns out that a lot of our clients look at those free postcards as 10,000 times $0.28 for postage. They started realizing, "Oh, my God, I'm going to have to mail 10,000 of these post cards! That's $2,800!"

All they saw was this tremendous cost, so what we thought was going to be a great benefit turned out to be a very negative thing. Again, you have to stay close to your customers, so you know how they're thinking. **Don't make any assumptions. Sometimes the way you *assume* they're thinking is not how they're thinking at all.**

Here's an example from my colleague Chris Hollinger. He sells a T-shirt showing a picture of our President running away from a calculator lady, because he's ringing up such massive debt. And it says, "There's something rotten in Washington. I think it's BO." Now, when Chris was thinking critically about making this offer, about mixing business with politics as this does, he thought that more than likely he was going to alienate many potential African-American customers. It seems logical, right? But the truth is, the response been absolutely the opposite. In the five months since he's launched this offer, he's had more people of color signing up with him than in his previous seven years in business. So Chris jumped to that conclusion erroneously.

And that's why this point is so important: **you not only have to think critically about your marketplace, you need feedback to be sure that you're on the mark.** That's what

Chris has done with his T-shirt idea, which is criticizing the President not because of his race, but because of his policies. That's a critical distinction. Now, he's gotten hate mail, which is another form of feedback. But the numbers don't lie. And that feedback you get from your sales team really helps you keep your finger on the heartbeat of your marketplace. Sometimes you get a surprise like this, when something you thought was going to happen is totally opposite of what does.

Sometimes it's for the better. Sometimes it's for the worst. Either way, that feedback is absolutely necessary.

$ $ $ $ $

CHAPTER TEN

You must be a BIG THINKER to make BIG MONEY!

✓ First comes the GOAL (the mission, the focus, the target).

✓ Then come the specific strategies you will use to achieve this outcome.

✓ The why to do something is far more important than the how to do something.

✓ Work backwards. Establish the goals and the game plan first — then develop the steps to getting there.

$ $ $ $ $

You Have to Be a Big Thinker to Make Big Money

Here's something that sounds like common sense—but as Mark Twain used to say, "Common sense is a very uncommon thing." **If you want to make big money, think big!** If you want to catch a whale, don't use a minnow for bait! **It's all straightforward: first comes the goal, the mission, the focus, the target.** Then come the specific strategies you're going to use to achieve that outcome. **Not only is *why* you do something far more important then *how* you do it, you have to start at the end and work backwards.**

Here's what I mean: you establish the goal and the game plan first, then you develop the steps to get there. Too many people are far too unreasonable when it comes to making money: they trip themselves up by trying to focus on the details before the concept. **Remember: concepts first, details last.** The goal always comes first. If you don't already have a written goal in place covering how much money you want to make, then you're shooting yourself in the foot. If you don't have one, your activities aren't going to be nearly as focused; you're not going to be as productive; you're never going to make the kind of money that you could. **So create that written goal, and set it high.**

When we first came up with the idea of making a million dollars a month, it was about twice the amount we were normally making. We set the goal, then we developed the strategies, then we looked at the necessary numbers. Similarly, we recently developed a $100 million business plan for a new company that we're starting. Well, that doesn't mean we're necessarily going to achieve $100 million worth of revenue a year; however, that's our business plan. **We're thinking big here—because it requires no more effort to think big than it does to think small.**

I used to listen to a motivational speaker who's no longer with us. He used to say, "You have to see it bigger, and think it simpler." **Most people just don't think big enough: they're thinking excessively small, simply not demanding enough from life.** Therefore, I would encourage you to set big goals, and not worry too much about all the details. **Most people get too bogged down in the details, when really, they should be worried about the broader concepts.**

Now, admittedly, frustration and confusion are going to be traveling campaigns on the road to success. There's no question of that. **There will be plenty of times when you get confused and frustrated.** That's one of the reasons why your goals have to begin with those big concepts. You have those things that you're always running towards; you have those ideals, if you will, **so anytime you do get frustrated and confused, you can always go back to those goals—you can always go back to those concepts.**

The founder of Domino's Pizza, Tommy Monaghan, went through a tremendous series of crises where he almost went bankrupt about six different times in his career. And the last time was the worst. He went through a period of two or three years when there was almost no light at the end of the tunnel. It looked like he was going to lose everything he'd worked so hard for. So one of the things he kept doing as a way of coping with all that, **and as a way of keeping him on focus and on target, was to spend hours going back to the basics of his business.**

He had 6,500 different franchises, and he would do things like running different cost analyses, just running the numbers on paper, proving to himself repeatedly that his ideas could work, and staying focused on that main goal. It's like when you're a race car driver or a jet fighter pilot. There are no rear-view mirrors: your eyes and attention *must* be focused on what's ahead. Same for the businessman. **You have to stay focused on the road ahead.** You can't avoid confusion and frustration, but you have to find a way to get beyond it; and **part of that is to keep going back to your goals and to keep thinking big.**

It does go back to laying out those guiding principles that are going to lead you through those rough times when you're bogged down in details, when you're overcoming obstacles, and you're caught up in the chaos of the moment. This helps you keep your eyes on the prize—and it can do the same for your entire organization. As Daniel Burnham said a century ago, there's no magic in little dreams. You're not going to motivate anybody—you're not going to push anybody to excel or to join you in any endeavor whatsoever—if all you want to accomplish is the little things. **You've got to have those big, exciting dreams that really get you going, which infuse you with energy that translates to your business, translates to your customers, translates to everything about you—not just in your business, but everywhere in your life.**

THE 2-STEP MARKETING SECRET THAT NEVER FAILS!

Thinking big, having those big dreams, those big motivations, really *does* more than just keep an individual focused. **It can stimulate an entire organization,** like the Tea Party political movement here in America. Their enthusiasm has been generated by the principles of the Constitution and responsible government. It resonates with people—but only because people got passionate about it, had a big dream. Look, we've got to do *something* here before our government crosses too many lines. At what point in our evolution of a civil society do we decide that's the case? This is something that people are afraid of, so there's a movement out there of people saying, "Look, this is enough. Let's pull our heads out of the sand and let's right the ship here." Something like that has to be bold and big to really get things done.

And when do you cross that line? Because there *is* a line. Anybody can *think* big. We can all sit around and talk about how many billions of dollars we want to make, but that doesn't mean any of us are going to make billions of dollars. **When does it become delusional?** That's the question I asked one of my mentors once: "When do you cross over the line, so that you're thinking so big that it's just foolish?" And he said, **"When you stop believing it, first of all, and when you're not willing to do whatever it takes. Because just having a huge goal isn't enough; it has to be followed up with the willingness to do whatever it takes to achieve it."**

One of the things that Chris Hollinger says is close to his heart at the moment is a software system that his company is creating. When his developers told him that their alphanumeric sequence and their servers would handle up to 60 million people, he was like, "Well, that's thinking big!" But it has to have that kind of number-crunching capability to calculate all the commissions. So when *you're* thinking big, what's a good number to shoot for? Would a million be enough? Chris has set some incremental goals for his first year, and those goals are going to drive his focus on how much advertising he's going to need. How much work is required, for him and his members, to recruit that many people? **Chris has some big goals, but they're concrete enough that he's going to be able to shoot for those goals and keep his eyes on the prize.** A year from now he wants to be able to say, "Look, we're doing what we set out to do," and at the same time know that it's now going to be easy.

Having those goals is important. **Set the bar high.** This inspires you to achieve more; and whether you achieve everything you tried for or not, it's still worthwhile to try.

CHAPTER ELEVEN

Business is an amplified lifestyle.

It's life amplified! We deal with <u>more</u> problems, challenges, highs and lows, good times, bad times, headaches and hassles, joys and sorrows <u>in one year</u> than most people live with in an entire lifetime.

Business is an Amplified Lifestyle

Business is life amplified. I like to say that it's life on steroids. We deal with more problems, more challenges, more highs and lows, more good times and bad times, headaches and hassles, joys and sorrows, in one year than many people deal with during their entire lifetimes. Business is an up-and-down, roller coaster situation; it can be extremely challenging in all its aspects.

The thing is, everybody wants all the good stuff, but they don't want any of the bad stuff that goes with it. **That's part of the reason why they don't give it everything they've got, part of the reason why they're not willing to do whatever it takes to succeed. They're trying to protect themselves.** They're trying to think smaller, because they don't want to bring on more problems than they can handle. **But come on, now: problems are a part of life!** I doubt that there's anyone over the age of 20 reading this who doesn't know that instinctively. Life is problems, and problems are life. **In business you get more problems, not fewer — and that's not a popular reality.** People don't want to hear that there are more problems in business than in regular life.

Look, anybody in America who wants to make millions of dollars can do it. *Will* most people do it? Absolutely not. They don't want to go into the dark places. They don't want to deal with the uncertainties. **They don't want the millions of dollars worth of headaches that you have to go through to make millions of dollars.** It's not worth it for them, and I understand that. Business isn't for everyone; those people need jobs. They want to punch in and punch out, so they can have some time away from work, which is fine. Because if you're an entrepreneur, business is with you all the time: It's a 24/7 thing, more like being a farmer than anything else. Farmers don't have time clocks.

I also think of business as a combination of art, war, politics, and sports, and maybe religion for some people. It's an all-encompassing thing, and a lot of people just don't get that, because all they want is the money.

I don't mean to sound negative here; but you have to realize that business really is life amplified, all the way around. **Sure, the problems are amplified, but so are the highs!** And it's certainly not for everybody. **One of the problems I see with a lot of business owners is the fact that they start working *in* their business and not *on* their business.** They wade in and try to handle all those little things that others can do just as efficiently and more cheaply, and they let those lows drag them down. There will always be obstacles standing in your way, folks.

Here's something that might help you be less negative about the amplified lifestyle. In the movie *Rudy*, there's a scene where Rudy's dad is telling Rudy, "Look, you're a Ruettiger. You're going to have to come back to the steel plant and that's going to be your life, by God." And yet Rudy wasn't going to do that. He had made up his mind, and he'd made a commitment to his best friend who died in the steel plant, that he was going to go out there and play football for Notre Dame. That was his goal, and it was a high, huge goal. **Most everybody in his life told him he wasn't ever going to achieve that goal. And yet he did, and of course it's a very inspirational story!**

Well, business has its own rewards like that, and there will always be those people in your life who will tell you that you can't do something. **Too often, you see people that succumb to that negativity.** They let it drag them all the way down. Well, part of being an American is pulling yourself up by your bootstraps and getting the job done! Oh, you can get down on yourself and wallow in self–pity about your problems, whether they're of your own making or other people are throwing them on you. But when it's your business, your baby, you have to pull yourself up or fail. Yes, those highs you find are exceptionally high; but even on the very same day, something else can happen to throw you in the doldrums. **All you can do is learn from that, move on, and keep striving to do the very best that you can.**

A failure to acknowledge that business is an amplified lifestyle will set you up for serious pitfalls later on. Business can be going along great, and then all of a sudden you get kicked in the gut. Well, that's life. How you respond to that says a lot about your character. **Whatever you do, though, don't set yourself up for more pain than you need.** Don't ever get caught in the trap of working *in* your business rather than on it. If you do that, eventually it's no longer fun. If you can't derive some other enjoyment out of it besides the money (assuming you get even that), then what's the point? **You need to love what you're doing, so you won't ever work a day in your life.**

When you can do that, life is fun. That's the game of it all.

CHAPTER TWELVE

Business levels the playing field. Anyone with a strong desire to get rich and the willingness to do whatever it takes — CAN GET RICH!

Business Levels the Playing Field

Anyone with a strong desire to get rich and the willingness to do whatever it takes *can* get rich. It doesn't matter what race you are. It doesn't matter what religion you are. As long as you're working in a free market, you can be of any race, creed, or religion. You can have any body type, be of any age. *None of that matters*, **because business levels the playing field.** You don't even need to be blessed with a high I.Q; you just have to be willing to do whatever it takes. All that business people have to do is focus on sales.

Here's a slightly off-color example that I've mentioned to Drew Hanson, my sales manager, before. I don't mean to offend anybody, but let's just say that there's this 478-pound telephone salesman working in our office. This guy's so fat that we'd have to build special ramps to get him into the building, and we'd have to wheel him in to his office. And let's also say that he has very poor personal hygiene. This is an extreme example here, but extreme examples are always the best ones. So let's really pile it up and say that he's also the world's biggest jerk. You get the picture, right? We have to put him in his own office, keep him away from the other salespeople. But let's *also* say that this person can sell one out of every two people he talks to; not only that, but he can upsell one out of three on some other thing. **This guy is the consummate salesman, creating the kind of revenues for Drew's sales department that none of the other** salespeople can touch.

That being the case, do we care that he weighs 478 pounds, has poor hygiene, and is a big, huge jerk who offends everybody except for the customers? Do we care if somebody has to wheel him into the bathroom, if he has special requirements? **Hell no, we don't care! Business is like that.** If you can produce results, it doesn't matter who or what you are, it doesn't matter what religion you are, it doesn't matter if you're male or female, it doesn't matter what your age is, it doesn't matter what your race is—none of that matters if you can produce results!

I think that business is the greatest thing there is. Everybody talks about how unfair things are, and how all these minorities are getting pushed aside and held down. You have all these groups that have chips on their shoulders, who think the whole world is against them. **Business levels all of that. Business knows no race, it knows no creed, and it knows no religion. It just doesn't matter; none of that matters.** It's very encouraging to know that right now on the Forbes 400 list, there are over a dozen people who started out broke. They started from poverty, and didn't even graduate from college. Now they're among the 400 richest people in the world. In this day and age, your net worth has to be one billion dollars just to have the Number 400 slot on the Forbes list. **I find the fact that some of these billionaires started dirt poor to be encouraging, because it's one proof of the leveling aspects of business.**

And it *is* a level playing field. There are so many things that we point to in the media that are negative or bad about our country, our political system, the divisiveness in our politics, and

120

all that — and yet in the United States we have this great mix of capitalism, representative democracy, and freedom that doesn't care where you came from, what color you are, what class you were born to. There's still so much prosperity and opportunity in this country; even with all the problems we have, it's better than many other places in the world today. Look at our nation's poor. What is considered poor in this country is considered well-off in many countries. In most households in our country today, even those that are officially below the poverty line, you still have a microwave, a TV, heating and cooling. **Yes, there are drastically poor people in our country; but still, opportunity absolutely abounds here.**

There's no reason for people to be broke in our country today. That may seem a blanket statement from the perspective of the poor, but the opportunities do abound. Does that mean we don't have problems? Of course our country has problems. Maybe more than ever before; maybe not. But we still have more prosperity and opportunity than just about anybody else on the planet. **We have a system that can still work to produce prosperity for people who are willing to work for it and get out there and get it done, regardless of race, color, creed, or social standing.** It's all because we have that business climate, and we have a system that promotes capitalism.

And this leads me to another favorite subject, which is short-term "obscene" profits. There are those in our political system today who want you to believe that there are rich people sitting out there on tons of money, and we need to tax them so that we can pay down this deficit or make sure that you get your free government cheese. But the people they're *really* wanting to tax are the ones who are hiring others. Have you ever gotten a job from a poor person? No. **And are profits obscene when they're yours? Of course not.** Now, I'm not talking about price gouging. Somebody who goes into a devastated earthquake zone and sells a gallon of water for $90, that's price gouging. But otherwise there's no such thing as obscene profits, especially when the profits are yours.

The equation is simple enough: when revenue exceeds expenses, you have profits. **And there's nothing wrong with profits: nothing at all, because it leads to prosperity, and it leads to more jobs.** It leads to a bigger economy. Now, it's easy to get worked up when you see able–bodied citizens sitting around milking off their parents or the government. I've got a problem with supporting that. I don't want my tax dollars to go to that, and I don't want my prosperity to support that. **Not to get on a rant here, but point is there's too much prosperity in America for people to be sitting around being sluggos.**

It's easy to look at the older people who say that we're getting soft, and we're letting our founding fathers and our forefathers down, and think they're just cantankerous old–timers who are maybe just sore and cranky. But think about it: maybe their American experience, and the wisdom that they're sharing in their own way, is important. Maybe a lot of us *have* gotten too soft. Maybe it *has* gotten too easy for us, and we need a wake–up call every now and then to bring us back to our roots—to bring us back to those areas where we're willing to pull ourselves up by the bootstraps, and work to build the life that we want instead of expecting it to be given to us. **You know what? That prosperity and that spirit is still alive and well, even though**

we have a lot of slackers in our midst. Maybe we need to stop giving those handouts to everyone, and make them work for it.

That's where business success comes from. **Business is work, hard work; and it works best if you work smart, too.** That kind of business does level all the playing fields. We hear so much about jobs, jobs, jobs, and how few are being created, and how many are being lost. Forget jobs. **More people should just become self-employed.** Where did we get this idea that it's all about a paycheck mentality? Not everyone is suited to be self-employed, but so many more of us are than most people think. God bless all the good employees, but still: a little bit of free enterprise goes a long way. In fact, I'll go out on a limb right now... and I don't mean to offend anybody. This is just my opinion, and I could be wrong: but I believe that free enterprise will save the world. I believe that countries doing business together will be less likely to want to kill each other.

You see, in business you can hate the people that you do business with, in some cases; but you still treat them with respect, and you try to serve their needs. You don't kill them. I think this is a solution for the world, and the world economy, and the whole future for thousands of years to come. **Free enterprise is good diplomacy, because you *need* to treat your customers with a certain amount of respect.** And even competitors who hate each other get together at business parties and other functions and manage to be civil with each other, no matter how jealous and envious they may be otherwise.

I love business. And you know, when I first started getting interested in business about 30 years ago, I read a lot of books about it, and they made it sound *so* complicated. They still do.

THE 2-STEP MARKETING SECRET THAT NEVER FAILS!

My God, I pick those books up and look at them and say, "What is this nonsense? This is ridiculous, this isn't a business." They make it so complicated... and truthfully, business is simple. **It's the simplest thing in the world! You're offering products and services that people want. You have your marketing, your management, and your margins.** It's so simple and so elementary, I wonder why they don't teach it to little kids from the time they can understand it—rather than forcing them to grow up thinking it's so damned complicated, when it's not.

Business is simple, and it levels the playing field. It doesn't matter who you are, as long as you can do a good job of selling. That's *all* that matters.

CHAPTER THIRTEEN

Ideas are slippery fish!

**They come in sudden flashes!
Write them down — <u>fast</u>!**

Ideas are Slippery Fish!

Ideas are like slippery fish: you have to hook them and pin them down right away, or they'll escape. They come in sudden flashes, so you have to write them down or otherwise record them immediately. **You have to grab every single one that comes your way, no matter how stupid or weird or unworkable you may think it may be... because sometimes, those are the very best ones.** You see, it all comes down to creativity.

I've discussed this before in other Ways. Look: people start off being so creative. When we're kids, we have so many great ideas! Little kids are all amazingly creative. We tend to lose that as we grow older and become focused on certain things. **But creativity is something you can work on: so sit down and brainstorm, take a lot of notes, come up with a lot of different ideas.** I keep legal pads all around my house. My staff gives me a Christmas gift every year, and this past year I told them I just wanted legal pads, because I was about ready to run out and I needed a few cases. I know I'll put them to work. It'll be the gift that keeps on giving all year, because I write ideas down constantly.

Why do I do that? Because, again, quantity leads to quality. **The more ideas you have, the more *good* ideas you have.** Professional photographers sometimes have to take hundreds or thousands of pictures before they find one or two that make it into the magazine or onto the website. Same with ideas: the more the better. And your best ideas don't come when you're sitting on your ass, either, unless you're sitting on your ass working on your projects, generally behind a computer. **They come when you're actively engaged.** When you're in the thick of a certain project, oftentimes *that's* when your ideas for the next project will come to you.

Here's a quote that means so much to me that I want to repeat it, even though I've mentioned it in other Ways already. Remember, confusion and frustration are part of the game, but here's the quote: "You go as far as you can see, and then, when you get there, you can see even further." **Your best ideas will come to you as you're moving forward, going as far as you can see, putting things together.** When you get past one hurdle there will be all these new ideas and you'll wonder, "Where were they before?"

It's a process: You just keep moving forward, working on your business, not in it. **Just come up with ideas, and learn what works best for you.** One of the things that works best for me in terms of generating ideas is sitting in the shower drinking coffee, as I've mentioned elsewhere. (It's a little silly, I know, but that's okay: if it works for one person besides me, it's worth sharing.) When I wake up in the morning, the first thing I do is make myself some coffee. The second thing I do is turn on the shower. Then, I'll sit in the shower drinking my coffee, letting the hot water hit me, constantly thinking.

I'm thinking about my projects, I'm thinking about the different ideas I'm working on—and I need answers. I'm confused about some things. I'm frustrated about other things. And you know, the answers do come to me. Creativity is a magical thing; some of these ideas just seem to appear out of the blue. **But they really do come, because you're working on lots of different projects; you're thinking consistently, you have lots of different pieces of the puzzle put together, and then all of a sudden, *Bam!*** They come together into some great ideas.

All you need at any particular point is just enough ideas to keep you moving. You don't have to have some grand five-year or ten-year plan for your business. All you need is a three-month plan, or even just a 30-day plan. Again, it's like driving at night. If you can see 50 or 100 yards ahead of you all the time, you can drive hundreds of miles with no real problem.

You never know when that next great idea is going to hit you... and if you don't capture them, they *will* escape. **I know that for a fact, because there have been times when I haven't written down great ideas, and I've lost them.** They've happened in the middle of the night or in the shower, for example, and I couldn't write them down. Chris Hollinger tells me he's even written stuff in the steam on his bathroom mirror when he didn't want to forget it and didn't have anything to write on. He's even gone back there and steamed up the bathroom again, just so he could see what he had written! And then, of course, the idea comes back to him.

Have you ever had one of those times in your life were things were just clicking? You were learning something brand new, and it was exciting, it was fresh, and your mind was on fire? That's something that happens in the amplified life of business. **These ideas come to you, and maybe you can apply them and maybe you can't; but you write them down just the same.** That's a good habit to have, whether you end up ever implementing them or not.

Right now, for example, Chris Hollinger and his wife are creating a brand new program, as I've mentioned; they've been putting a lot of energy into that, and Chris tells me that his wife has been coming up with a lot of outrageously crazy ideas. Some of them are fantastic; they might have nothing to do with their business, but if they could apply them, man, would that be cool! And is there a market for some of them? Yes, there is. So she's going through this phase where she's writing down all these ideas that she wants them to try. **Maybe she and Chris will get around to implementing some of them; maybe they won't.** But she's having a good time coming up with them, and the thing is, if you don't write them down then they're gone forever. They're slippery critters.

And again, the more ideas you have, the more good ideas you have. **Just think about that: quantity leads to quality.** Try to get on the other side of the cash register. Study what other people are doing with their marketing; steal ideas. You know, one of the reasons that I've been so impressed with Mr. Hollinger is that he's a great student of the field. He and people like him look around and see all these possibilities, and they take a little bit from here, and a little bit from there, and so they incorporate the best ideas that other people are using into their own business models.

That's very, very smart. You see, ideas aren't copyrightable. **If you find an idea that somebody is using, and it's a good idea, then find a way to use it yourself; find a way to make it better.** Never plagiarize, but do find a legal and ethical way to copy others.

CHAPTER FOURTEEN

The greatest entrepreneurs tend to be the worst managers. The skills it takes to build a business are usually the opposite of the skills it takes to manage it.

The Greatest Entrepreneurs Tend to Be the Worst Managers

I learned this one the hard way... well, I learned *all* of these things the hard way, but this one in particular! And here's what I learned: **that the skills it takes to build a business are the *opposite* of the skills it takes to manage it.** My wife Eileen is a great managerial-type business person, and I'm not. But I didn't know that at first. The entire 14 years that she ran the company, from 1988 through 2001, I always thought I could do a better job. I kept it to myself for the most part, but that's what I believed.

And then, after she stepped down for health reasons, I tried to run the day-to-day operations for about two and a half years—and it was the worse period of my life. **I found out the hard way entrepreneurs can be good in some roles, but bad in others.** Pure entrepreneurs have strengths; they do serve a vital role, especially for growing businesses. But once the businesses are mature, entrepreneurs are basically useless in the day-to-day handling of the fine details. **They're terrible managers.**

It takes certain skills to bring in money, you see. But those skills are usually the *opposite* of the skills it take to manage. One of the reasons my wife is such a good manager is that she's the queen of stability. You could set your watch by the woman; I often know what she's going to say before she says it. She's just so stable, so consistent, and *those* are the kinds of qualities it takes to run a business from day to day. **The qualities it takes to bring in all the money are more entrepreneurial: the skill of the salesperson, the hunter.**

So when it comes to making money, getting it and keeping it require two completely different skill sets. I had to learn that the wrong way. You see, entrepreneurs tend to be wild—eyed dreamers, kind of crazy people. They're not known for their stability, necessarily, and when it comes being a good manager that quality is absolutely necessary. I spent two and a half years of my life learning this one the hard way.

Yet so many people are trying to wear all the hats in their businesses, which causes some big problems. They're trying everything in their businesses themselves. Now, a good business is sort of like a clock. Think of an old-fashioned timepiece, where if you take off the backing you can see all the gears working away in there. Some of those gears are big and some are small, but you take out any one of them, the whole thing quits working. It could be the tiniest, cheapest gear in there, and if you take it out, the mechanism stops. **That's how a business is. It requires different talents from different people working together to create synergy. It's a team effort.**

I think my friend Chris Hollinger's business is a good example. He tells me his wife provides certain things that he lacks, the same as with Eileen and I. He says she's generally the stabilizing influence—the rudder to the ship, whereas he's the motor boat. She's trying to steer a stable, straight course for their enterprises. And he says that they work as a team not only in their business, but in their marriage as well. Her skill set compliments his, filling in where he's lacking, and vice versa.

That's been a benefit to their business, and it's a great model for what I'm talking about here.

You see, **a successful business must include someone with the skill set and the mentality of a creator and motivator, the person who has all the ideas and can get themselves and others motivated to achieve those ideas. And then there's the person who can contribute substance and structure and stability to an organization, as well as discipline when that's necessary.** I'm talking about financial discipline especially. It's rare that you find someone that can do *all* of that in business, which is why I feel that my earlier gear analogy is appropriate here.

Part of becoming successful is becoming aware of your limitations, so that you can work around them. You need to be willing to go out and find the people you need to counter your limitations, and team up with them so that you can acquire the skill sets you don't already have on your side. No one is perfect in and of themselves. There was once a Roman emperor, Marcus Aurelius; he was godlike within his empire, but he was smart enough have a servant who followed him wherever he went to tell him, repeatedly, "You're just a man." That's all the servant did; his job was to keep Marcus Aurelius grounded.

So be willing to acknowledge the fact that you might not be good at certain things. I know a lot of people (men in particular) who have trouble acknowledging that fact, and it's always to their detriment—in their personal relationships as well as in their businesses. **I say, your greatest strength is to know your weaknesses.** When you know your weaknesses, you can delegate tasks to people who are strong in the areas you're weak in. That's what a business is: a team. **It's a synergistic effort of people who come together for mutual benefit, and each has their role to play.** Together, all the people on the team are smarter than any one of them, and that's a very powerful thing.

Also, you have to consider the reality that, in a way, every strength is a weakness. People who are very strong in one area are often weak in an opposite area. And yes, the people who are really good at something make it look so easy. That's why for 14 years, I thought I could kick my wife's butt at being a business manager: she made it look so damn easy. That's what happens when you find people who are good at anything, **so find the most talented people that you can find. Recognize that if you're strongly entrepreneurial, you're probably a lousy manager.**

Don't waste years of your life, like I did, finding that out.

CHAPTER FIFTEEN

The best stories to use in your sales material are **before-and-after stories**.

This is a powerful sales formula. The story tells about the problem and then it introduces the solution. Next it shows the great life-changing benefit. *The reader puts himself into the story and is sold!*

The Value of Before-and-After Stories

The best stories to use in your sales material are before-and-after stories. **This is a powerful sales formula, because it first outlines the problem and then introduces the solution. Next, it shows the life-changing benefits, in such a way that the reader is able to put himself or herself into the story, which allows them to be sold.**

I want to start this section by talking about stories in general; then, I'll give you a few examples of how we use stories as part of our ongoing marketing effort at M.O.R.E., Inc. **I'll tell you about the one story that's made us millions and millions of dollars, and continues to work and will *always* make us money, no matter what.** This is another of those secrets that really is a secret, because it's obvious that most people just don't get it... and even those who do often aren't using it to their fullest advantage. Heck, it's possible that we don't either. Though we certainly use this formula a lot, we could probably use it even more than we do.

While the best stories are before-and-after stories, stories in general do an amazing job of letting people put themselves into the picture you're painting. It lets people use the power of their imagination. People remember stories, because stories touch them emotionally. **They help people understand complicated issues, too, since we're all trained to**

listen to stories. The truth is, nobody really *wants* to listen to your sales message. The last thing people want is to be sold something. But they do want to hear stories; they'll happily listen then, because they enjoy them and have been listening to them since they were kids. **Their sales resistance is lowered.** That's why all of your sales messages have to be buried within the story. It's a method of soft selling.

As a rule, people have this invisible shield they put up around themselves. You can't see it, but it's very real. **That shield rejects most sales messages because, quite frankly, they're trying to hold onto their money.** They know you're trying to pitch them something, and they don't want to be sold. **That's why you use stories to explain complicated things, to make it easy for people to want to listen to the advantages and benefits that you have to offer.** You do it as a way of breaking the ice a little. People are uptight when they know you're giving them a sales presentation, so a nice story relaxes them and it lets you do an effective job of selling. Just like every other skill, you can get better at it with practice.

Here are some examples of how we use stories. Let's start with something very recent. Chris Lakey and I are getting ready to introduce a whole new type of opportunity to our clients. We came up with a name for this opportunity that's built around a story that we want to tell. The name of the opportunity is the "$400 Million in 72 Months Secret," or at least I think that's probably what we'll call it. **Because people want to hear secrets.** They don't necessarily want to hear a *plan*, but they definitely want to hear secrets! This opportunity is built around the story of a company in New York that was started 72 months ago, and has already generated over $400 million in revenue. We tell the story, and then we show them how the new opportunity we're inviting them to be a part of offers many of the same advantages—yet, it's different and better in some ways. **By using this story of the 72-month success, we're able to tie our opportunity in with their opportunity.** That's one of the great things that a story allows you to do. **It's easy for people to remember, and it has the honesty of credibility along with it.** Again, you're able to explain one thing by comparing it with something else.

People like stories. They like hearing about extremely successful companies that have discovered something incredible. **They want to hear all the inside facts, and that's exactly what we're going to give them. But what we're *also* going to do is wrap it around our new opportunity and show people the comparisons, and how what we have is even better.** I hope you can see how this story gives us a great way to present something new, by talking about something that's 72 months old and has a history of real success. By calling our opportunity by the name of our story, people will remember it. They'll remember that "$400 Million in 72 Months," because people do remember stories.

Here's another example of how we use stories on a day-to-day basis. We have a special business within our business called our Five Star Mailing Service. We create and send out direct mail postcards and small direct mail letters for our clients. **We sell that service by telling people about our own success with direct mail.** We tell them the story about how we first got started with space ads in national magazines, then met Russ von

Hoelscher six months later. Russ helped us go from making $16,000 a month to almost $400,000 a month, by giving us the best of the best of his secrets. **We tell people that out of all of those secrets, the one that's made us more money than anything else is direct mail marketing. Then we talk a bit about the $100 million in total revenue that we generated in our first 19 years alone**—again, primarily through direct mail marketing. **Next, we tell them about our Five Star Mailing Service, which incorporates the best of everything we've learned since we first started using direct mail back in 1989.**

People remember this story. It's a before-and-after story; before we started direct mail, we were bringing in about $500 a day, or $16,000 a month. After direct mail, we were generating almost $100,000 a week, within nine months of Russ getting us started. That's easy for people to remember, and it helps drive the point home. **Direct mail is a powerful way to make *millions* of dollars. We've done it, so we've got the credibility, the knowledge, and the experience that our clients need if they want to do what we did.** That story has been very, very helpful to us.

We've also got a special project we're putting together right now called our ATM websites. **ATM is an acronym for "Automatic Transporter Method," but we also tell people it's the next best thing to having their own money machine—so it was only appropriate to call it the ATM.** We show them a picture of the ATM machine at our local bank. We talk about how great it would be if you could own your own personal money machine, and this just helps people to fire up their imaginations.

You see, that's part of what makes stories so wonderful.

People listen to them, and then they see things in their own mind's eye. Their imagination kicks in. If you're just trying to preach at people, their minds might wander off in another direction. They might tune you out. **But by telling them a story, their brain becomes engaged and alive, and they get with the plan, so to speak.** They get excited and the emotions kick in, so you're able to sell them without them realizing they've been sold. And that's very important, because while people like to discover and buy things, they want to think of those discoveries as their own discoveries, as if they're making these important breakthroughs on their own. **Nobody wants something pushed down their throat; they'll resist that. In order to sell people, you have to break through that resistance.**

The principle we call the Four Cornerstones of Wealth is another way we use stories to help sell things. I won't go into them here, except to say that we tell people that there are four things you need if you want to get wealthy, and then we proceed to use visual analogies in a construction sense — where cornerstones are an important part of a foundation. **But then we also tell people the story of how we've used all four of those things to get rich ourselves.** This helps them assimilate that knowledge better, and it makes the principle more credible. **People are open and receptive to the concept.** We're making it easy for them to see that if they just had the same four things that we had, they could potentially have all the money that they want, too. That makes it really easy for us to sell those ideas. And then, of course, whatever opportunity we may be promoting, we show how that opportunity includes those four elements.

As you can see, we don't just start out by selling our

opportunity, or our products or services. **We start out with something they want to hear about, in this case the Four Cornerstones of Wealth.** They want to be educated a bit. **They want to find out what these four things are that they need to get wealthy.** That's how we start the presentation, and then we relate a story about how we had all four of those things in our own lives. This makes it so much easier for them, when it comes time to show them how what we're offering lets them tap into all four of those things. Their minds can grasp it now. **When people are resisting, they can't grasp anything.**

Incidentally, the way that you say something is often even more important than what you say. It's all about the presentation. **And that's what stories allow you to do: a much better job of presenting.** So let me tell you the story that's made us God only knows how many tens of millions of dollars. **It's the story that built our company, and it's the story that continues to make us money.** It's our rags-to-riches story.

For years, my wife Eileen and I sent away for every business and money making opportunity we could get our hands on. Our names were on all the mailing lists; everybody was sending us all kinds of plans. There were sales letters and ads and postcards for their plans coming in the mail every day, trying to convince us that they had the secret that could make us rich, if only we gave them enough money. For years we struggled; and it was frustrating, it was confusing. Our friends and family laughed at us, and told us we were foolish and crazy to think that we could get rich. And yet we refused to listen to all those naysayers. **We continued to believe in our dreams—and eventually, because we didn't give up, we found just the**

right combination of products and services and opportunities. Within five years, we had generated over $10 million in total revenue.

We tell our clients that they can do the same: that if they refuse to quit, if they'll just stop listening to all the naysayers in their life, if they continue to keep their minds open, they can have the same kind of success that we've had. **Heck, their success could make ours pale by comparison.** I've told that story thousands of times, in various ways. I know it instinctively; that story is a part of me now. And the reason I tell it so often to our clients is because it's the greatest before-and-after story I know. **They want to be in that story themselves; they identify with that story.**

They really *are* just like us. Their names are on all the mailing lists, and when they go to their mailboxes they pull out the same kinds of get-rich-quick sales letters and postcards that we used to. **Our story lets them bond with us.** It lets them identify with us. It builds a rapport. **It lets them see that it *is* possible if they just don't quit, like we didn't quit.** That story has been worth millions of dollars to us.

So think deeply about the value of telling stories. Think about the main selling points that you want to get across. When we started our multilevel marketing company, Club-20 International, we told all kinds of stories about the ways we were different from a traditional multilevel company. Each story represented a point of differentiation between us and the competition. **Comparisons, analogies, metaphors, and really good storytelling: these are the secrets to selling people who don't want to be sold, although they do love to buy things.**

THE 2-STEP MARKETING SECRET THAT NEVER FAILS!

Get good at it, keep practicing it, and stay aware of it—
especially when somebody's using a story on you.

Here's a story that's been worth a billion dollars—literally.
It's a two-page sales letter that earned the *Wall Street Journal*
over $1 billion in revenue. It simply told a story about two
young men who graduated college, with both of them equal in
every way. But one of these young men subscribed to the *Wall
Street Journal*, and the other did not. And now, 20 years later,
the subscriber is a multimillionaire and the other one is a mid-
level manager—a Dilbert-like character who's nameless,
faceless, just an average Joe. People liked that story; they
remembered it, and it made the *Wall Street Journal* a fortune.

Copywriter after copywriter tried to beat that letter—and it
was the control at the *Wall Street Journal* for many years,
because no copywriter ever could. It may sound a little stupid—
**and yet we're talking about how important emotions are,
and how to drive your message right into the heart of that
emotion, and there's nothing that does it like a good story.** So
think about the story that generated millions for our little
company, and then think of that story that generated over $1
billion for the *Wall Street Journal*... and think about ways that
you can tell emotional stories, too.

To reiterate the original point, **the best stories to use in
your sales material are before-and-after stories.** That's
basically what the *Wall Street Journal* story is. This is a
powerful sales formula. The story describes the problem, and
then it introduces the solution, and next it shows the great life-
changing benefit, therefore putting the reader in the story, where
they can see getting the result themselves.

146

One of the former vice presidents for Walt Disney, Alan Kay, has said this: "Why was King Solomon recognized as the wisest man in the world? Because he knew many more stories or proverbs than anyone else. Scratch the surface in a typical boardroom, and we're all just cavemen with briefcases, hungry for a wise person to tell us stories." Before I even found that quote, I was already thinking about stories being used historically, and immediately one of the things I thought about was storytelling in the Bible. Those stories have influenced our culture for thousands of years. **But storytelling has been around for much, much longer than that; ever since there's been a story to be told, there's been someone there telling it.**

People who have knowledge, who have learned a lot or have a lot of personal experiences, have a lot of stories to tell. Someone lacking in experience doesn't have many stories. When you look at a young child versus an older person, there's a big difference in the stories they tell. A high school kid's experiences are very limited in scope. They don't have many responsibilities. They haven't lived much life so far, and the stories they're able to tell are very minimal. On the other hand, someone who's lived a long life and experienced a lot, who's traveled the world—they've seen a lot of things. They've got a lot of stories to tell. **So your stories have a lot to do with how many years you've lived, and how much you've experienced during that time.**

A fellow named Lawrence Shapiro once wrote a book called *How to Raise a Child with a High EQ*, where EQ is emotional intelligence. At one point in the book he says, "Many people don't realize the extent to which stories influence our behavior, and even shape our culture. Think about how Bible stories teach the fundamentals of religion and rules of conduct. Think of the fables and parables that molded your values. Think about how stories about your national, cultural, or family history have all shaped your attitudes about yourself and other people." As Shapiro points out, **we really take these stories to heart. They become a part of our life experience, a part of who we are; they're in our cultural DNA, really.** Some stories, of course, aren't that important to us; when we hear one like that, it doesn't have much impact. But there are other stories that have a lifelong impact, and they really do shape who you are.

So again: getting back to the original intent of storytelling for sales purposes, **you want to use stories to relate to people, to get them to understand the before-and-after of the benefits of using your product or service. The stories that will result in the most sales are life-impacting stories.** In our business, we sell business opportunities and help people make money from home. Well, we know that our marketplace is looking for life change: they're looking for something that can have a dramatic impact on their lives, so a story about someone else who experienced the results they want to experience will stick in their minds. **They want that story to be *their* story.** They're already somewhere in the story, actually. Maybe it's a story about someone who didn't have success and struggled for years, and then finally achieved success; they see themselves in that. They become a part of the story, and they want the solution—e.g., the end result that you shared with them in the story.

This is especially applicable if the story is a true one. Now, there are different kinds of stories, such as fables or parables, that aren't real— but they're useful because they illustrate a point. That said, **the very best stories to use when you're trying to sell a product or a service, and promising a certain benefit or solution to a problem, are true stories about someone else who achieved the results that your prospect is looking for.** That makes it easy for the prospects to see themselves receiving the benefits the person in the story received, so they want to jump into the story themselves. **In short, the story helps the prospect internalize and personalize that benefit.** They want to be that story, and that makes them more interested in responding.

Western writer Louis L'Amour once said, "A writer's brain is like a magician's hat. If you're going to get anything out of it, you have to put something in it first." I thought that was an interesting quote, because with a magician's hat, of course, you're not *really* going to just pull a rabbit out of nowhere. That's not real. A magician's hat has to be filled with the rabbit before the rabbit can come out. **As a writer, your goal is to fill your brain with all kinds of experiences that enable you to tell the stories you tell.** If you've never filled it up, if you've never read a lot, if you've never experienced life, then you're going to be lacking in the story department.

So be sure you're well-read at least. Even if you don't like to read, try to read a lot of biographies. Read about people who've done things and achieved success, especially in your specific marketplace. Even those secondhand experiences will become valuable stories for you to tell as you craft sales letters, as you sell from a platform, or do phone-selling. **Anytime you're face-to-face or one-on-one with a prospect, you've**

got the ability to use stories to make the sale. Your writer's brain, your storytelling brain, your sales brain, is a lot like that magician's hat in L'Amour's quote. To get something out of it, you've got to put something in it first.

Here's another great quote, this time by Mark Twain: "Don't say, 'The old lady screamed.' Bring her on and let her scream." His point is that the more dramatic you can be with your stories, the better. **He's saying, don't just talk about something: make it *real*. In your storytelling, be as descriptive as possible.** You may not actually be able to have a lady there screaming, but you can describe it as best as you can. Use very colorful, descriptive language as you describe the events of the story. **Don't be boring!**

You've probably been in situations where you're sitting around a table or you're at dinner with people, and there's a story being told. Then, someone else jumps in who says, "No, no, no, you're telling it all wrong." Then they proceed to tell the story their way. It's the same story, but one of them is telling it in a boring way, and people are sleeping. The other one says no, no, that's not how it happened, and then they tell the same story—and everybody's laughing and wide awake. They're hanging on every word. What's the difference? **Simple: one person was telling the story in a straightforward, unexciting way, and the other person was livening it up, using lots of adjectives and describing things in full detail.** He was laying out exactly what was happening, and making people hang on every word. **That's the power of good storytelling: getting people to want to pay attention to what you're saying.**

In the book *The Art of Storytelling,* Nancy Mellon points

out that because **there's a natural storytelling urge and ability in all human beings, even just a little nurturing of this impulse can bring about astonishing and delightful results.** As I was reading that quote, I was thinking about kids. Chris Lakey has six of them, and they're all great storytellers. Kids do tend to be storytellers, even though they lack experience. They've got stories that are true and stories that are all in their minds, and they're very real either way. They'll tell you the story in full detail. As we mature, though, a lot of us lose the ability to tell good stories. We've lost that natural urge. I think that's what Nancy Mellon was talking about. Just a little nurturing of this impulse can bring about astonishing results.

So as you think about writing sales copy, remember that being a good copywriter, just like being a good salesman, is a skill that can be developed. In a similar way, storytelling is something that can be nurtured. You have the ability to practice the art of storytelling by telling lots of stories. The first thing required is to be knowledgeable: to have lots of information, lots of inputs into the brain. **Mixed with life experience, that becomes the foundation of the ability to tell stories.** The natural storytelling urge is there. You just have to nurture it, to get that ability to pull a story out of your hat to become a part of who you are. That way, there's always something there, for every situation.

The writer Studs Terkel once pointed out, **"People are hungry for stories. It's part of our very being. Storytelling is a form of history; of immortality, too. It goes from one generation to another."** People are *hungry* for stories. They love telling them, and they love hearing them. Whenever you're sitting around with family or a bunch of your buddies, you're telling stories, right? You're just sitting there having a good time, telling stories. Stories are a part of everybody's daily life. We all tell stories. We're either telling them, or we're listening to them. It's a part of our social fabric, our social DNA. It's how we pass things on from one generation to another. I know stories about my family's history because my parents told them to me. We know about our history as a nation because people have passed down stories and written things about our great-great-grandparents and how they fought in this or that war, how they overcame this or that or didn't, whatever the case may be.

That desire, not only for people to hear stories but for people to tell them, should become a part of your ability to make sales. **As people read or hear your stories, they identify with you; it builds a bond.** People laugh over stories, they drink over stories. Sometimes they cry over stories. That storytelling builds a bridge; it builds a connection.

Chris Lakey sold cars for about a year, once. One of the things they always teach you in car sales is to get the person talking about who they are—get them telling stories. Find some common ground. Do you like doing something they like doing? Do you both enjoy playing golf? Is there some hobby you're both interested in? You can't know until you tell some stories and build a bond with the prospect. **They'll like you and trust you faster if you have stories to build that bridge than if you don't.**

The writer Robert Fulghum came up with something called **"The Storyteller's Creed," which I feel is appropriate to this discussion. It goes like this: "I believe that**

imagination is stronger than knowledge. That myth is more potent than history. That dreams are more powerful than facts. That hope always triumphs over experience. That laughter is the only cure for grief. And I believe that love is stronger than death."

Who knows how widely accepted that is among storytellers? But it's interesting to think about, especially those first three statements. "I believe that imagination is stronger than knowledge. That myth is more potent than history. That dreams more powerful than facts." So imagination, myth, dreams, and stories are stronger than knowledge, history and facts. When you talk about these things, you're talking about parables, or fake stories. You're not talking about true stories. Think about the fables of Aesop, or the parables in the Bible. The goal of these stories is to make an important point. **The right example, related through a parable, can be more powerful than facts or knowledge.**

So, instead of spending all your time and your sales copy spouting off numbers, talking about facts and other things that make people full of knowledge, spend some of your time telling stories. **Spend your time talking about the way things could be, or the way things *should* be.** You're encouraging people to daydream, to imagine receiving all the benefits that this product will deliver on. You're saying, "How would your life be better if you used this product? Let's dream a little." That kind of imagination in storytelling can help you make more sales, because you'll build those bonds with your prospects a lot faster. **They'll trust you more quickly, which lays the foundation for you to makes more sales.**

THE 2-STEP MARKETING SECRET THAT NEVER FAILS!

Again, we're talking especially about before-and-after stories, which can be real or fictional, depending on the point you're trying to get across. If your story's fictional, that's fine, as long as you tell people it is. Don't try to pass something off as real when it's not; make it clear you're using a parable or fable. But don't hesitate to use true stories to make the point that your prospect is experiencing a certain unpopular or painful experience, when they could be receiving the benefits and the results you're promising them through your offers. **It's the way things are now and the way things could be, or *should* be, that you're trying to explain to them.**

So remember: your brain really is like a magician's hat, as odd as that may sound. To get anything out of it, you've got to put something in it first. **You've got to have a lot of experiences to pull from.** Either read up on other people's stories, or live the adventure yourself. You've got to have stories to tell, so you can sell more stuff to more people for more profits. And once you have those stories, how do you use them? Well, there's a popular copywriting formula called the PAS formula.

PAS is an acronym that stands for Problem, Agitate, Solution. The Problem is the pain that you remind people they're dealing with. A, you agitate the problem—you make it hurt more as you force them to face it head-on. And then the S is when you introduce your solution to that painful problem, whether that's a product, service, opportunity, your company, or yourself. **When you get on the other side of the cash register and start thinking like a marketer, you'll see all kinds of individuals and companies using this very simple formula.** In TV commercials, you see it frequently, especially if they're direct response marketing commercials. You see the actor frustrated about something; maybe they have to chop up all these vegetables by hand, and they're crying because of the onions. That's the problem. Then they agitate the whole thing, trying to make it personal, before viola! They introduce that solution.

That's what you do when you write copy: you try to tell stories. **Stories help to agitate the situation.** Again, they slip under the radar, and they become personalized, internalized. That's what the agitation process is. And then you reveal the solution. When using that PAS Formula, simply write down the main problems that your product or service or company or *you* solve, and then think of as many different stories as you can that help to illustrate that problem, which is the agitation part. **You're wanting them to put themselves in the picture.** Only once you've done that do you introduce the solution.

When we tell people our million−dollar story, we talk about all of the pain and frustration we went through. That's part of the agitation, because again, our clients are going through that same type of thing themselves. They're frustrated, they're confused, they're looking for solutions, and they're not really finding them. **By telling them our story, we agitate things and make it all real for them.** Again, you have to subject yourself to a lot of different sales material to see how other people are using this. But stories are just amazingly powerful. All of the great religions are built on stories. Politicians use stories all the time.

And let's take a closer look at that. Politicians love to bring up stories of certain people who supposedly represent the kind of person who's struggling with the same issues that they're

THE 2-STEP MARKETING SECRET THAT NEVER FAILS!

promising to help overcome. Joe the Plumber was a big one in an election a while back. Just some guy named Joe who was a plumber, and they just started picking up his story. Everybody started using that to try to illustrate how they could solve these problems that Joe the Plumber was having. You see politicians do that all the time, because it helps to personalize things.

And you see it in the news all the time. In fact, the news is really just one story after another. That's all. And I don't necessarily enjoy watching the news; I have lots of problems with it, personally. But my wife watches the news, and since I live in the same house she lives in, I'm constantly around it. And I watch her. She likes watching the news, and she gets pulled emotionally into these stories. Every night during the news, at least one time, my wife is crying. Now, she doesn't sit there and bawl, but she's crying. **These stories are reaching her emotionally.**

They're part of what being alive is all about, those emotions. If you take the emotions out of life, there *is* no life. **Stories are emotional things, and people love hearing them for that reason.** Imagination and dreams and myths and love and drama: all those are emotional things. Those are all things that tug at the heartstrings. **And you must never forget that people buy emotionally; so that's how we have to reach out to them, just as the news does.** All those great stories help connect us with people.

There are a several shows that Eileen and I watch that are supposed to be news shows, but they're really not. They're soft news, like *Dateline* and *48 Hours* and such. Well, my Mom watches those shows, too. I talk to my Mom on the phone several times every week, and these stories help give us something to talk about. It's a connection we have: we both watch the same story, and now we can talk about it.

So think about that. **Stories are a part of our lives, every single day. And the people who are the greatest communicators are often the greatest storytellers.** Case in point: a friend of ours, Russ von Hoelscher. He's one of the best storytellers I've ever met. He just has a way about it. Whether he's consciously developed those skills or not, I don't know; but I do know that some people seem natural at it, and are just better at it than others. Ross has certain stories that I've heard him tell maybe a dozen times or more, but I always like to hear them, and I'll even encourage him to tell the stories again.

For example: we were in Dallas, Texas in August 2010 for our Wealth Explosion seminar, and we were all eating lunch together. After lunch, things hit a bit of a lull and the conversation ran dry. So I said, "Russ, tell the story about this. Tell the story about that." He loves telling stories, as I think all good storytellers do. They wouldn't be good if they didn't enjoy it. Ross enjoys getting everybody to laugh, and his stories are full of dramatics and details. **Again, that's the kind of thing that helps you put your prospect in the picture; it helps them see things and remember the story better.** It's human nature to want to keep hearing the same stories again and again, because they're fun to listen to, especially if they're related to subjects that are of interest to you. In this case, in Dallas, we were there with a number of speakers, and the speakers who hadn't heard Russ' stories before really enjoyed them. Everybody wants to be around a great storyteller.

That's why your job is to be a great storyteller, so you won't be one of those people who just bores everybody to death—the kind of person where, when you walk in a room, everybody's trying to avoid you. Nobody can stand being around you because all you do is talk, talk, talk, without ever saying anything imaginative, creative, or fun. A great storyteller, they're also talking nonstop—and yet what they're saying is fun to listen to, it's exciting, and you just can't seem to get enough of it. All the great entertainers are great storytellers; they have to be, because storytelling is a part of entertaining. **And people want to be entertained more than anything.** That's why the richest people in the world, except for some CEOs, are entertainers.

One of my mentors is a consultant, and I've paid him well over $100,000. He's worth every penny; he's helped me a great deal. And in hindsight, one of the reasons I've paid him so much money is that he's an amazing storyteller. I know probably 20 or 30 of his stories that he's told me or that I've learned from some of his audio programs and his books. **They're great stories. I remember them, and they're all stories that mean something to me. They all make a point that's helped me.** I'm convinced that one of the biggest reasons I've paid this gentleman so much money over the years—for various seminars, and consulting, and coaching groups that I've been a part of, and the books and all that—is because he's an amazing communicator with an incredible ability to tell stories.

That doesn't happen by accident. Some storytellers make it sound so effortless, and yet, they've spent countless hours thinking things through and working on their delivery. So don't let them fool you; otherwise you might be intimidated, thinking, "Oh my God, I'll never be able to tell stories like that." But you can. **Think things through and look for things that are dramatic, things that will stick in people's brains, and use them in your sales copy and pitches.**

Stories influence people. They get people to do things that they wouldn't normally do, had it not been for the story. Let's look at one of those stories Russ told back in Dallas; it's one of his best, and I'd heard it before. In fact, I've mentioned it before in the 500 Ways! After we had lunch on the first day, Russ said, "T.J., before this event is over, I need to tell you about a really important project that can make both of us a lot of money." And I said, "How about right now?" Because I didn't know what was going to happen, given the rest of the schedule. We might both get really busy and lose track of it.

There was another speaker in the room. He said, "Oh, I have to go do something, anyway." He left the room, and Russ told me a story about a lady he met 15 years ago who had an idea for a product. He was speaking at a $5,000 event, and at break time, after his presentation, she came up to him and she showed him this product she had. He didn't think it was that good, and he started trying to discourage her just a little. He gave her a couple ideas for selling it, but his whole theme to her was, "Keep your day job." And she said, "No, Russ, you don't understand. I've already sold over a million and a half of these." That blew him away.

And then he proceeded to tell me how the moneymaking idea he was proposing was even better than the idea that this lady had profited from. And once he told me that story, I saw what he was saying, and how it could be true. It was all speculative, of course; but he was using her example to try to explain something else. That helped me immediately see the possibilities, whereas if he had just told me about this product, I wouldn't have been nearly as influenced or excited about it. It would probably have just gone in one ear and right out the other. **But by using that great story about her trumping his discouragement with her obvious success, and then him showing me how his idea is even much better than that, he was able to draw me in.**

I hope you can see how great an influence that one idea had on me, because it caused me to go into overdrive immediately. We spent a lot of time and money and energy putting together a product line based on this idea, because that one story influenced me to such a great deal. **I bought into it... and likely I wouldn't have, without the story.** So think about that. Think about how stories affect all of us on an everyday basis. The next time you get excited because somebody presented something to you, stop and think about what they did to get you excited. I'll bet they used a good story, or a metaphor, or an analogy. They tried to explain something by comparing it to something else. That stuck in your mind, you saw it immediately, and you got all fired up.

And again, think about your own life. **The best stories to tell are your own.** There are things that excite you, so share them. Part of selling to people is a transference of emotion. You're excited, so you get *them* excited. The best stories pump you up, jazz you, get you enthused. **You can then build whatever it is you're selling around those stories in order to**

get other people excited.

This "$400 million in 72 Months Secret" that Chris and I are launching: I learned about this story during the Thanksgiving holiday. When I read about that company in New York that generated over $400 million in their first 72 months, man, I got excited about it! And when I told Chris about it, *he* got excited, and he started seeing possibilities that I'm convinced he might never have seen had I not mentioned that story to him. So think about your own life. Think about the stories that *you* have. **Think about what makes you excited. Those are the best, most powerful stories that you can tell to get other people excited, too.**

I honestly believe that the more people add good, solid storytelling to their marketing, they more they're going to profit. Depending on your model, you may experience a very dramatic increase in your sales and profits just by mastering the art of storytelling—by finding ways to incorporate more stories into your sales presentations, whether that's by direct mail or face-to-face, and especially when you're selling via the platform. In all things that you do selling-wise, adding storytelling can dramatically improve your bottom line.

There's a saying that the heart rules the mind, and that's why we must sell to people's emotions. **That's what storytelling is all about, really: the heart ruling the mind.** When you're selling, you're generally appealing to emotions; and again, storytelling speaks directly to those emotions. Think about how emotion–driven the entire selling process is. When you see a commercial on TV, they're appealing to your emotions for why you need this product, not your intellect. When you get an offer in the mail, or you respond to a catalog, or you visit a website and you see something, they're trying to tap into emotion.

Now, some purchases aren't always or aren't completely emotionally-based; buying toilet paper is a good example. But even then emotion creeps in. There's a reason people buy squishy Charmin instead of the thin, cheap generic stuff. It's because people see the persuasive commercials on TV, such as the ones with the bears (at least as I'm writing this), where they're using the squishy toilet paper and having a pleasant experience, instead of a harsh experience using the rough toilet paper. **You'd think that the necessities of life wouldn't be sold emotionally, and sometimes they aren't—but often they are.**

Think of the commercials for Axe, the body wash and deodorant. They're totally sexualized, aimed at either the high school or college−age crowd. They want you to believe that slapping on some deodorant will make you sexy to the people who are attractive to you. All of a sudden you're going to be a magnet to all these hot women or men, when all you did was take a shower with Axe shower gel and apply some Axe deodorant. **So they're appealing to your emotions, not the rational, logical part of your brain.** The rational part of you says, "I don't need to spend six bucks on a product for the shower. I could spend $2 and get the same result. Both get me clean. One might smell one way while another one smells slightly different, but they'll both do the job." **Well, the emotional part of you doesn't believe in this.**

And it goes beyond that. Consider cars, for example. Why would someone spend $40,000 on a car when a $15,000 car will still get you from point A to point B? It's the emotions that go into car buying that influence that decision—whether you want this brand over that brand, or you want one that has a leather interior and dual climate zones and a DVD player that drops down in the back and a GPS in the front and a six—disc CD changer, and all the features that go along with making a decision on buying a car. **It's all emotional, and I think that's what we're talking about here with storytelling.** Stories reach people at a deep emotional level, a level you can't get to just by arguing features or facts of numbers, or by being detail—oriented about the specifics that go into your product.

If you don't appeal to emotions at a psychological level, you'll never get someone to buy from you. If they're just going on facts and figures, then there's almost certainly going to be something out there that can do the same thing more cheaply. It may be more efficient, or it may appeal to them more on the factual level. **But when you reach deep and use stories and appeal to the heart, that will always win out.** People will spend more money for something they really, really want than they will for something they really, really need. So appeal to emotions. Appeal to the heart. Use lot of stories and lots of examples to sell. Use your own story. **The ability to tell your own story is critical to your success.** There's nothing more effective than your own example of what happened when you yourself were doing whatever you're trying to illustrate in the story.

Earlier, I mentioned politicians using stories. **They do it because they know it tugs at the heart.** It doesn't matter than there are 300 million people in the U.S., and this one person is the only person they could find who has this problem; by pointing him out, they make people feel like it's a widespread problem... and they can pass legislation that puts tight restrictions on something, because one person got up in front of Congress and had a sad story. That's why they use stories.

The fact is, stories are everywhere; everybody tells stories. It doesn't matter who you're talking to or what the scenario is, whether it's just buddies on the golf course or someone on a platform selling a product, or whether it's a waitress in a restaurant—or whatever the situation is. We're using stories as a part of life. It's time *you* used stories to sell your products and services, if you're not already doing so. It's just an extension of what you're already familiar with, what you're already doing. **Make a calculated effort to use stories to present your case for why your prospects need to do business with you.** As I'll outline in more detail later, the heart rules the mind. That's why we must sell to emotions. Storytelling will get you to the heart, and that's why you want to use them as often as you can.

And try to use as much enthusiasm as you can when you tell your story. I know some people who *try* to tell stories, but they drone too much. You don't want to be one of those people that everybody's trying to run away from when you come walking in. When you go to a party and you're looking around and you see an animated conversation happening, where people are enthusiastic and are waving their hands and laughing and that kind of thing, you naturally want to gravitate there. That's because people respond to emotions. So tell your stories with force. Tell them with enthusiasm. **Be as dramatic as you can.** Look for as many examples as you can. Extreme examples often help; they stick in people's brains. A good joke is a good story, too.

Just try to become a better student of this kind of thing. **The better you get at it, the more money you can make; because, again, nobody wants to be sold anything.** People hate to be sold stuff. **But people *do* like to buy stuff, and so it's our job to make them think they're buying instead of being sold.** The best marketers are those that sell you without your knowledge of it, so it's all right under the radar. They're using a lot of stories. They're getting to you emotionally, causing you to think that you're the one who actually sought them out, that you're the one who's buying from them, rather than them selling to you... although, quite honestly, the reverse is probably true. You wouldn't buy from them if you didn't have an interest, that's for sure.

Nobody can ever sell you something that you don't want. **But people can sell you all day long without you even realizing it when they're using the powerful principle that I've discussed in this chapter.**